DECISION SYSTEMS THEORY

JUAN MARTÍN FIGINI

authorHOUSE®

AuthorHouse™
1663 Liberty Drive
Bloomington, IN 47403
www.authorhouse.com
Phone: 1 (800) 839-8640

Translated by Cecilia Hirschler Fernández.

Published by AuthorHouse 11/26/2018

ISBN: 978-1-5462-6710-2 (sc)
ISBN: 978-1-5462-6709-6 (hc)
ISBN: 978-1-5462-6708-9 (e)

Library of Congress Control Number: 2018913278

Print information available on the last page.

This book is printed on acid-free paper.

CONTENTS

ACKNOWLEDGMENTS

There was a person who accompanied me through the entire process of bringing this work to life. Her name is Cecilia Hirschler Fernández, and she happens to be my wife. Thank God we found each other, and she did not hesitate in following me in this innovative project with positive implications. All the graphics, some examples, and part of the order were invaluable, time-saving contributions. Whenever I finished developing a section of the theory, I asked for her analysis and reflection. I am deeply grateful to have shared this work with her, and that her related tasks contributed to the accomplishment of this great goal.

Thank you very much for helping me to develop this work. Thank you for this great act of love and generosity.

And I always thank God and all his servants for being with me in every step I take. Sometimes I make mistakes, but I examine them and rectify my behavior. Thank you for all the lessons and challenges that I have experienced and will experience. Thank you. You help me grow. You help me mature.

INTRODUCTION

Freedom is a faculty of the soul that enables the possibility of choosing among different options of manifestation.

In other words, freedom is the faculty of the soul that manifests itself through the act and effect of choosing.

Choosing is the mental action through which human systems determine the options of manifestation, which are restricted or enabled by certain endogenous and exogenous factors, and they select the one they consider the most valuable according to their structure of preferences.

Decision is the act and effect of deciding. To decide is a synonym of choosing.

The decision systems theory is a set of concepts and laws that contribute to explaining the mechanisms and cognitive processes through which human systems value and evaluate their reality in order to choose among the different options of manifestation they contemplate.

When the (individual or collective) human system executes a behavior, it has already chosen. The decision made is manifested in the behavior, which is the corporal action. The question is: which criteria do human systems follow in order to choose the behaviors they execute?

The causes of origin of the decision are related to the mental system and, specifically, to a belief subsystem which is the decision system.

The **decision system** is an entity that justifies its existence and functions as a whole through the interaction of the valuation system and the viability evaluation system. The inputs are (internal and external) stimuli, and the outputs are decisions.

The decision systems theory seeks to explain why the multiple and different types of behaviors that human systems can develop are generated in certain circumstances.

It is important to clarify that this theory can be applied at an individual or collective level; in other words, it can be used for the study of conditioned decision making processes of individual and social human systems.[1]

The human systems, at a micro and macro level, make decisions that affect reality according to their particular decision systems.

Decisions are based on two previous mental processes: the determination of the options of manifestation and the valuation of the options. The first one is conditioned by the viability evaluation system and the second one by the valuation system, which are both beliefs subsystems that are part of the mental system. Throughout this book, we will explain the different variables that interact to generate the choices that define all human systems' lives.

---

[1]   In order to understand collective decision systems, we suggest to read the *Social Systems Theory. A model based on Mental Systems* (see the section "Related works" at the end of this book).

THE HUMAN SYSTEM: REALITIES AND WAY OF LIFE

The human system

The decision systems theory is built on the basis of the mental systems theory.[2] The latter offers a model of the functioning of the mind and its relationship with the soul and the body, developing a set of concepts and laws that seek to explain the mental phenomena.

It states that the mental system, and more specifically its belief subsystem, is the key to understanding the causes of the thoughts, the emotions, and the consequent behaviors of human beings and the communities they form.

Considering what has been studied through the mental systems theory, in this book we will analyze the factors that guide human systems in the decision making process. In other words, why do human systems choose certain options of behavior and not others? What laws influence decision making?

In the next pages, we will review the most basic notions of the mental systems theory, to which we will add some new concepts, in order to guide

---

[2]　The *Mental Systems Theory* was published by the author of this book for the first time in English in the year 2012, and its new and expanded edition was published in the year 2018. From this point forward, whenever we mention the *Mental Systems Theory* we will be referring to the version of the year 2018.

the reader in some fundamental definitions that will be used throughout this book.

It should be noted, however, that the complete reading of the mental systems theory will be of great help for all those who wish to widen their understanding of the decision systems theory.

Let us start by defining the human system:

The **human system** is an entity that justifies its existence and functions as a whole through the interaction of the soul, the mental system, and the body system.

An **individual human system** is a human being. A **collective human system** is a social system (or community), constituted by two or more individual human systems that interact with each other.

The term **protagonist** will be applied to the human system that is being analyzed.

From now on, when we refer to a human system, we can assume that it is an individual or a social system.

Likewise, when we use the concept of **person**, we will be referring to an individual person or a social person. The **individual person** is an individual human system endowed with an identity. The **social person** refers to a collective human system endowed with an identity.[i]

---

[i]   **Translator's note:** A human system may be individual or collective; and if it is individual, it may be of any gender (depending on each case study). As a convention, throughout this theory, we will use the singular pronoun "it," and its corresponding possessive form "its," to refer to a generic human system. In the examples, we may use the pronouns he, she, or it, depending on the person we are portraying. The gender of the protagonists in the examples has been chosen at random.

The **soul** (or will) is a conscious energy that enjoys free will and operates on the mental system and on the body system. The soul has two fundamental faculties: consciousness and free will. Consciousness is the ability to recognize the processes of the mental system and the body system. Free will is the ability to choose among different options of manifestation.

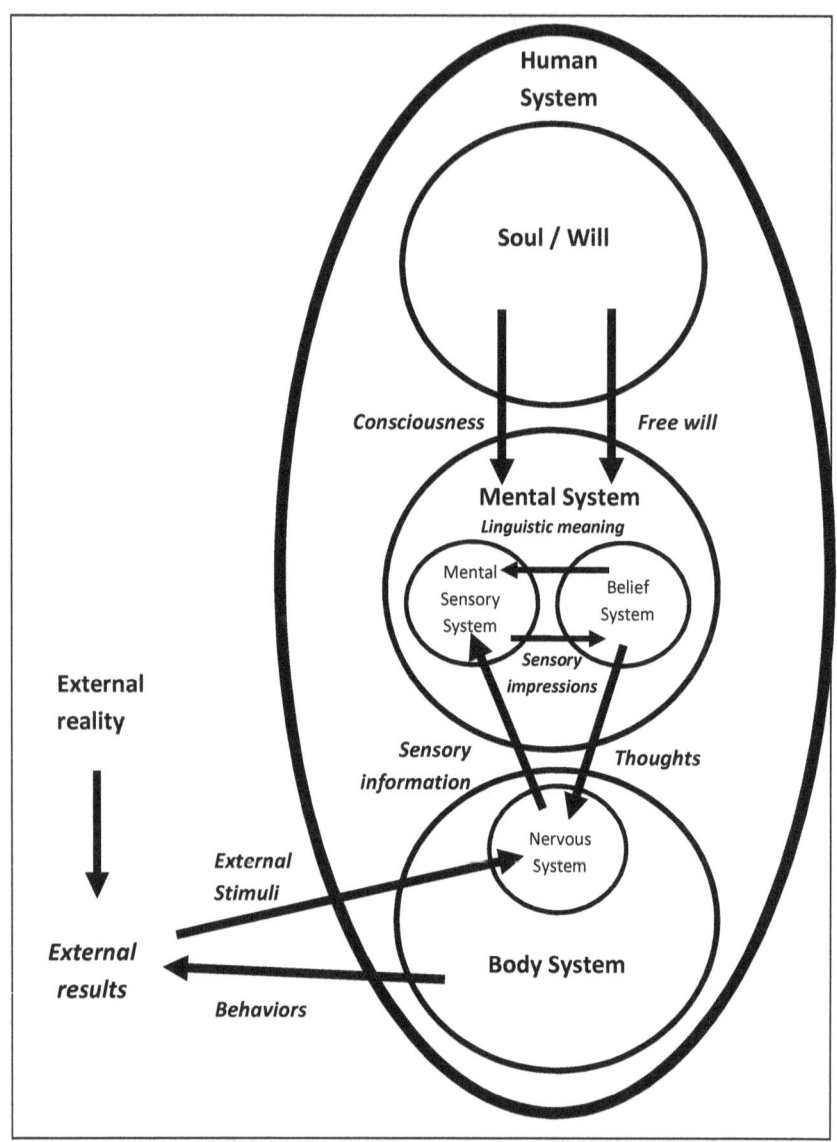

Figure 1: Human system interacting with the external reality.

The **mental system** is an entity that justifies its existence and functions as a whole through the interaction of the mental sensory system and the belief system. The input of the mental system is sensory information and the output are thoughts.

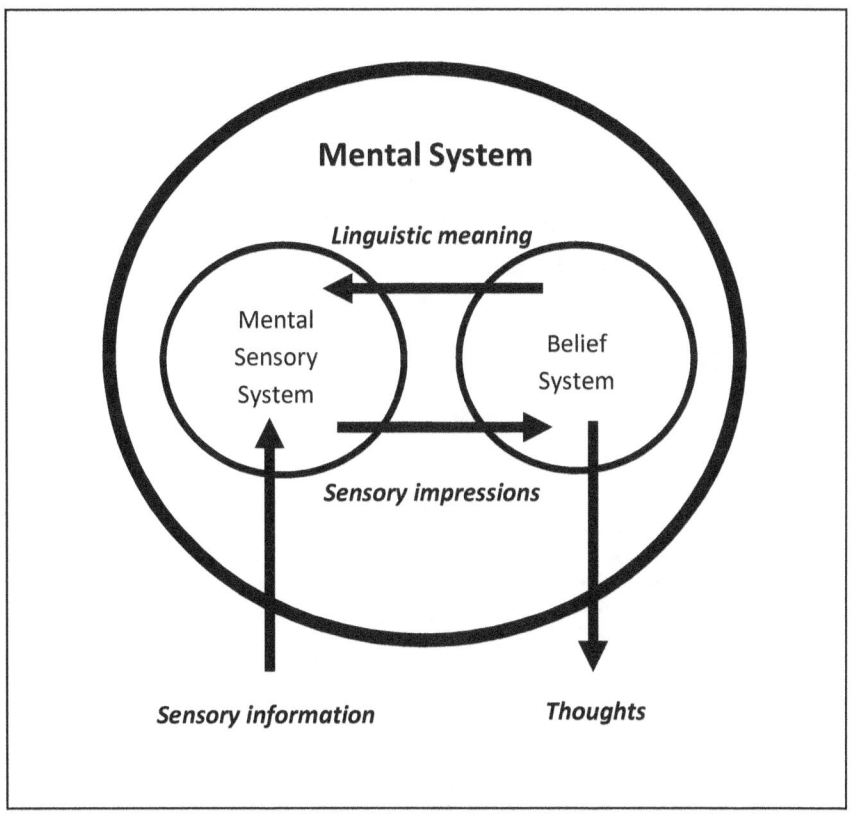

Figure 2: Mental system.

The **mental sensory system** is an entity that justifies its existence and functions as a whole through the interaction of the auditory, visual, tactile, olfactory, gustatory, and internal sensitive subsystems. It is responsible for generating **sensory images** (or sensory impressions), which may have an external or internal origin. In the first case, the images are a product of the sensory information that has been captured from the environment by the senses of the biological system of perception. In the second case, the images can have a physical origin (information received about the internal functioning of the body system) or a mental origin (thoughts).

Then, the emergent property of the mental sensory system is a sensory image that is immediately captured by the belief system. The **belief system** is an entity that justifies its existence and functions as a whole through the interaction of beliefs.

Beliefs are ideas that have a certain energetic charge and intensity and possess a certain degree of veracity. Ideas are sensory images with a certain linguistic meaning.

Beliefs are constituted by four variables: energetic charge (pole), energetic intensity, sensory images, and linguistic meaning.

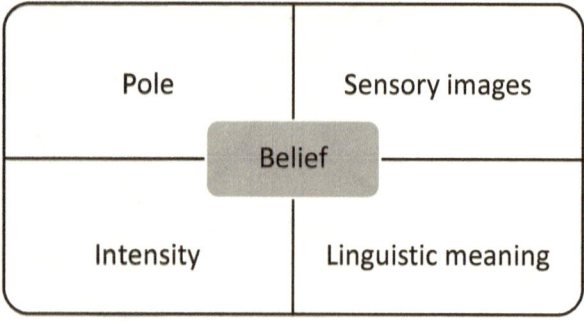

Figure 3: Elements of a belief.

The **linguistic meaning** is a coherent grammatical articulation in accordance with the human system's operative language. The operative language is the one used by the human system to perform every basic operation of reasoning. In general, it corresponds with the language learned in the early years of the human system's life.

Sensory images are mental sensory reproductions based on the senses of the biological system of perception. They are the emergent property of the mental sensory system, and we refer to them in plural because they are produced successively, enabling the capture of movement and change in the perceived reality. This uninterrupted reproduction enables the human system to have a kinetic sensory record, in other words, to perceive life as a movie.

The energetic charge of a belief is its energetic **pole**, which can be either positive or negative. The pole is positive when the belief is linked to the idea of acceptance. On the contrary, the pole is negative when the belief is connected to the idea of rejection.

The energetic **intensity** is the amount of mental energy that a belief contains. For explanatory purposes, we will use a scale from zero to ten points to measure the intensity of each belief (zero means no energy, and ten refers to the maximum amount of energy).[3]

Beliefs can be divided into active and passive beliefs. **Active beliefs** are all the beliefs that have an effect on the thinking process. Passive beliefs are in a potential state and, for that reason, they do not affect the thinking process.

Beliefs are connected to each other by certain logical principles, forming **associations of beliefs**. These associations, which are responsible for generating certain thought patterns, form belief subsystems.

Logical principles are ideas that guide the development of information in accordance with certain rational parameters. These parameters constitute norms of reasoning that enable the gestation of different types of associations of beliefs.

Multiple, combined logical principles intervene in every association of beliefs. For example: the principle of definition, the principle of identity, and the principle of cause.[4]

Active belief subsystems are entities that justify their existence and functions as a whole through the interaction of associations of active beliefs. Belief subsystems have the specific function of generating certain thought patterns. These subsystems are, among others, the conservation

---

[3] The parameter of measurement and evaluation used in this theory is a possible analysis tool. This parameter can be replaced, if it is wanted, by a model of evaluation more appropriate for a better record of the studied mental experience. For example, instead of assigning absolute values, we could apply a system of percentages.

[4] This subject has been briefly explained in the book *Mental Systems Theory. New and expanded edition*, and it will be elaborated in the book *Educational Systems Theory. A model based on Mental and Social Systems* (see the section "Related works" at the end of this book).

system, the linguistic communication system, the institutional system, and the decision system.

The **active belief system** is an entity that justifies its existence and functions as a whole through the interaction of the active belief subsystems. The input are sensory impressions, and its emergent property are thoughts.

The active belief system defines the human system's **personality**.

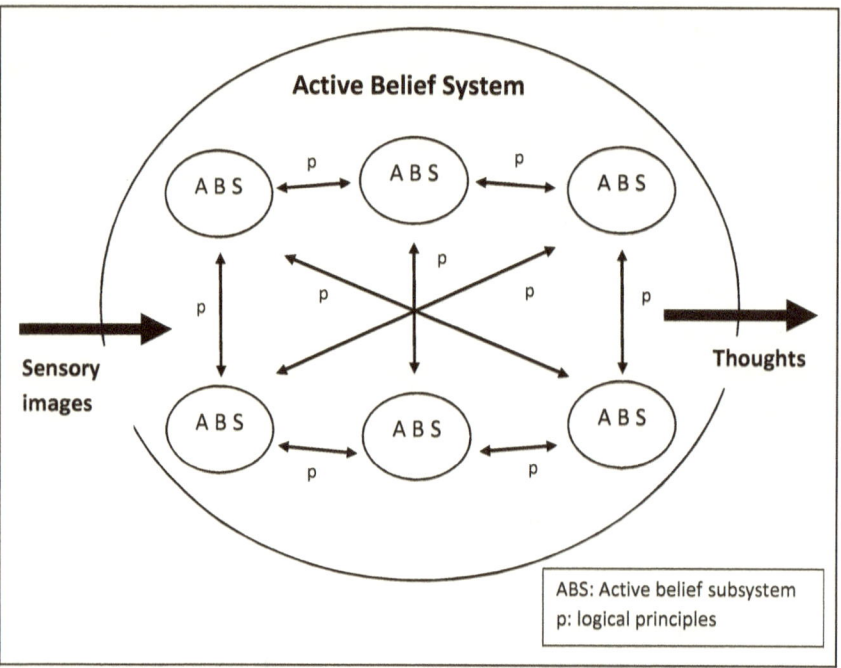

Figure 4: Active belief system.

The sensory images that enter the belief system are decoded by it and, as a result, thoughts emerge.

Thoughts are ideas that possess a certain energetic charge and intensity and affect the body system.

Each thought is constituted by the same four elements that form beliefs: pole, intensity, sensory images, and linguistic meaning.

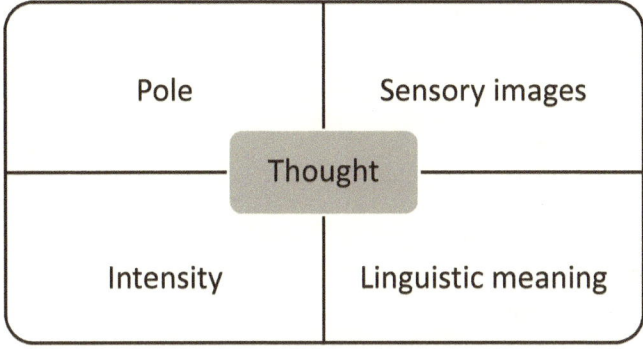

Figure 5: Elements of a thought.

The main difference between thoughts and beliefs is that the first ones directly affect the body system, while beliefs do not directly affect the body system. In addition, beliefs are part of a network, while thoughts are not. They are, instead, the emergent property of that network.

Thoughts generate multiple effects on the body system. One of those effects are emotions.

Emotions are physical sensations generated by thoughts. Emotion is a synonym for feeling. To feel is the act of recognizing bio-sensorially the structure of the thought.

The structure of a thought is formed by its constitutive elements: sensory images, linguistic meaning, pole, and intensity. This structure determines the type of bio-sensorial recognition that the body system will make and, therefore, the type of emotion that the organism will experience.

According to the law of correspondence, positive thoughts generate positive emotions, and negative thoughts generate negative emotions. Also, the law of proportional intensity states that the energetic intensity of the emotion is equal to the energetic intensity of the thought that generates it. For example, if the energetic intensity of the positive thought X is eight, the emotion that it generates will have a positive pole and an intensity level of eight points. In the same manner, if the negative thought Z has an intensity level of three points, the emotion it generates will be negative, with an intensity level of three points.

Thoughts are the causes of emotions. Thoughts and emotions are the causes of behaviors.

Behaviors are corporal actions (physical and/or linguistic) that affect reality.

The sequence that we have just described is summarized in the **law of human manifestation**: there is a certain order of manifestation that starts with beliefs and ends with behaviors.

Beliefs are the causes of thoughts. Thoughts are the causes of emotions. Thoughts and emotions are the causes of behaviors. The levels of this sequence are called **levels of manifestation**.

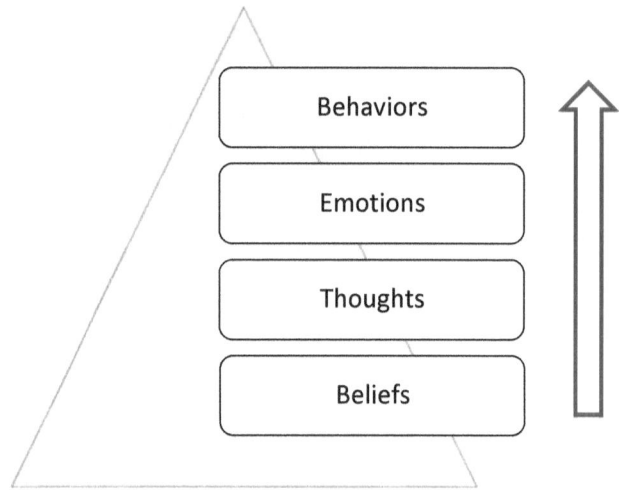

Figure 6: Levels of human manifestation.

In order to illustrate these concepts and processes, let us take the example of a person who is sitting in a room having breakfast.[5] Her biological system of perception is capturing a series of external stimuli with her biological senses: the visual image of the room with the window closed, the aroma and taste of the coffee, the sound of the cup against the table,

---

[5]   For didactic purposes, all the examples listed in this book constitute an oversimplification of the complexity of the phenomena that this theory seeks to explain.

the internal physical sensation of the heat from the coffee, the temperature of the environment.

These stimuli are transmitted through her cerebral system to the mental sensory system; which decodes the information it receives, through its sensory types, and transforms it into a series of mental sensory images that are captured by her belief system.

These sensory images generate a resonance with the belief "it is hot in this room," assigning that linguistic meaning to the set of images. Since the belief system is constituted by a structure of interdependent beliefs, the entering sensory impressions also generate resonance with a set of associated beliefs, such as "I cannot stand the heat" and "when it is hot, I am uncomfortable." As a consequence, from the interaction of this group of beliefs, the following thought emerges from her mental system: "I am uncomfortable," with a negative charge of a certain level of intensity.

That thought enters her body system, where her emotional system emits the emotion of "annoyance" (with a negative charge of a level of intensity that is equal to the level of intensity of the thought that generated it), which drives the individual to execute the behavior of opening the window.

As a result, a breeze of fresh air enters the room, which constitutes a new external stimulus that the person will decode.

We see in this case that the behavior performed by the person, the results generated by that behavior, and the emotions she felt were the effect of the way in which her belief system decoded the stimuli and the thoughts that it emitted as a consequence.

In the example, we have oversimplified the phenomenon, since there are other series of intermediate reasoning cycles that lead the human system to execute that behavior. In this sense, the thought "I am uncomfortable" and the corresponding emotion of annoyance entered the mental system as a new internal stimulus, where it was decoded again by the belief system, resonating there with the beliefs: "the window is closed," "it is a nice spring day," "a fresh breeze enters from that window in the springtime," "if I let the breeze come in, I will feel better," etc. As a consequence, from the interaction of this group of beliefs, the following thought emerged from her mental system: "I'm going to open the window."

All the behaviors carried out by a human system obey to certain thoughts about the future.

According to the **law of manifested behavior**, all the corporal actions manifested by a human system are the consequence of projective thoughts and commanding thoughts that enable them.

Projective thoughts are thoughts about the future that anticipate the action that the human system will execute (for example: "I'm going to open the window," where the person sees herself performing that action). **Thoughts that command behavior** are responsible for ordering the body to execute a behavior that materializes the projective thought. In other words, they order the body system to execute the desired behavior, which corresponds with the action visualized in the projective thought (for example: "open the window").

It is worth remembering that the human system is only aware of a small fraction of information about the multiple and diverse thought patterns it generates.

Behaviors produce a specific modification of reality. Any modification of reality generated by behavior is defined as **result**.

Reality is the set of phenomena that happen. From the point of view of a human system, reality may be of an **internal** nature (when it happens in its mental or physical system) or **external** (when it happens in its environment).

An external result is any modification of the external reality (environment) generated by behavior. An **internal result** is any modification of the internal reality generated by behavior.

Furthermore, results can generate new stimuli for the sequence of human manifestation.

All stimuli, of internal or external origin, are shaped by each human system's active beliefs through the decoding process. In turn, all thoughts, emotions, and behaviors are a consequence of certain associations of active beliefs.

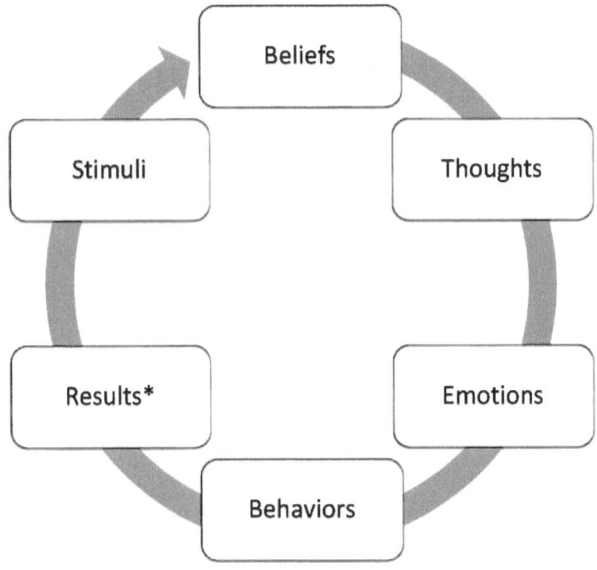

Figure 7: Sequence of manifestation-results-stimuli.

*The human system is only partially responsible for the result, since the latter emerges from the interaction between the human system and reality.

Types of realities and stimuli

Reality is the set of phenomena that happen. From the point of view of the human system, it can be divided into non-perceived reality and perceived reality.

Non-perceived reality is the set of phenomena that happen and are not sensorially captured by the human system.

Perceived reality is the set of phenomena that happen and are sensorially captured by the human system.

Internal reality is the set of phenomena that happen within the human system. Internal reality can be divided into internal mental reality and internal physical reality.

Internal mental reality is the set of phenomena that take place in the mental system.

Internal physical reality is the set of phenomena that take place in the body system.

External reality is the set of phenomena that happen in the human system's environment. The **environment** is the external reality with which the human system interacts.

Conscious reality is the set of phenomena that are perceived and recognized by the human system.

Unconscious reality is the set of phenomena that are perceived but not recognized by the human system.

It is worth noting that the distinction between conscious and unconscious reality is only applicable to the perceived reality, since the human system is always unaware of the non-perceived reality.

The distinction between different types of realities facilitates the analysis and the classification of the phenomena and stimuli that affect the human system. However, it is important to clarify that the perceived reality always happens in the mind, since all the sensory images that constitute it happen in the mental system (even though their origin may be external). For the human being, events are mental experiences of the internal or external reality, because the sensory images that define them are elements of the mind.

Throughout this book, when we mention the concept of reality, we will only be referring to the reality perceived by the human system.

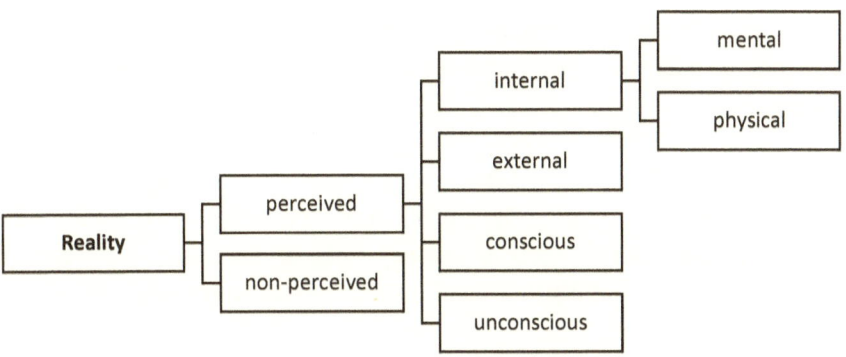

Figure 8: Types of realities.

Perception is the act and effect of perceiving. To **perceive** is to capture the events of reality through the use of the senses.

Individual perception is the sensory capture of the events of reality that is carried out by an individual human system.

Social perception is the sensory capture of the events of reality that is carried out by a social system.

The perceived phenomena of reality constitute sensory information that can also be referred to as sensory stimuli.

The stimulus is the act and effect of stimulating. To stimulate is to incite a system to produce a certain effect.

Sensory stimuli are unified fragments of sensory information perceived by the receiving human system that come from its internal or external reality and trigger the gestation of sensory images.

Individual sensory stimuli are unified fragments of sensory information perceived by the receiving individual human system that come from its internal or external reality and trigger the gestation of individual sensory images.

Social stimuli (or social sensory stimuli) are unified fragments of sensory information perceived by the receiving social system that come from its internal or external reality and trigger the gestation of social sensory images.

Internal stimuli are unified fragments of sensory information perceived by the receiving human system that come from its internal reality and trigger the gestation of internal sensory images. There are two types of internal stimuli: mental stimuli and internal physical stimuli.

Mental stimuli are unified fragments of sensory information perceived by the receiving human system that come from its mental reality and trigger the gestation of mental sensory images. They may also be called "thoughts."

Internal physical stimuli are unified fragments of sensory information perceived by the receiving human system that come from its internal physical reality and trigger the gestation of internal-physical sensory images.

External stimuli are unified fragments of sensory information perceived by the receiving human system that come from the external reality and trigger the gestation of external sensory images.

Unconscious stimuli are unified fragments of sensory information perceived by the receiving human system, which trigger the gestation of sensory images that are not recognized by the person (also called "unconscious sensory images").

Conscious stimuli are unified fragments of sensory information perceived by the receiving human system, which trigger the gestation of sensory images that are recognized by the person (also called "conscious sensory images").

The human system becomes aware of all the received sensory stimuli (both internal and external) in its mental space. All sensory images happen in its mind: the ones perceived with the biological senses and the ones remembered or invented

The acknowledgment of the perception of reality happens in the mind.

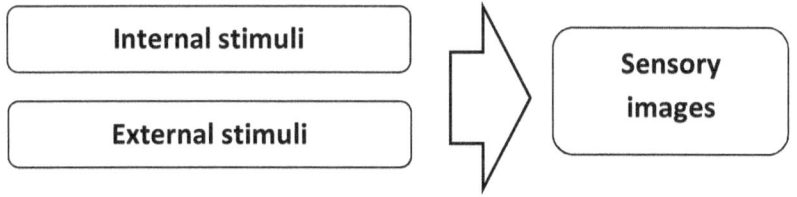

Figure 9: Origin of the sensory images.

Way of life: endogenous and exogenous systems

The **way of life** is defined as the set of constraints and resources which respectively restrict and enable a human system. It is a confluence of endogenous and exogenous factors that define the human system's lifestyle.

The **endogenous factors** are the set of constraints and resources, originated in the human system's internal reality, which respectively restrict it and enable it.

The **exogenous factors** are the set of constraints and resources, originated in the human system's external reality, which respectively restrict it and enable it.

There are different types of endogenous factors that constitute different types of endogenous systems. Likewise, there are different types of exogenous factors that constitute different types of exogenous systems.

The endogenous systems are the ones that define the human system's internal reality.

The exogenous systems are the ones that define the external reality that affects the human system.

A human system's way of life is determined by the interaction of the endogenous systems and the exogenous systems that constitute it and affect it.

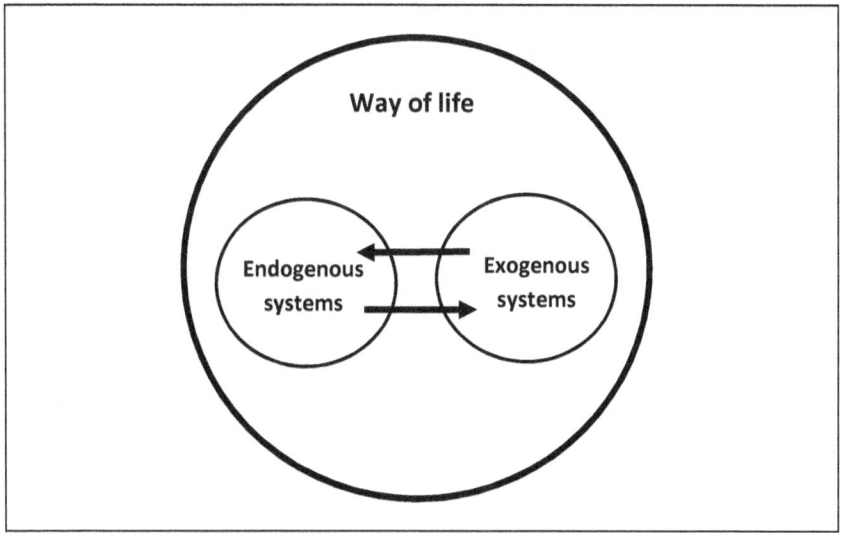

Figure 10: Human system's way of life.

In the group of the **endogenous systems** (which can be defined as the global endogenous system) we find the fundamental entities that constitute the human systems' internal reality: the will, the mental system, and the body system.

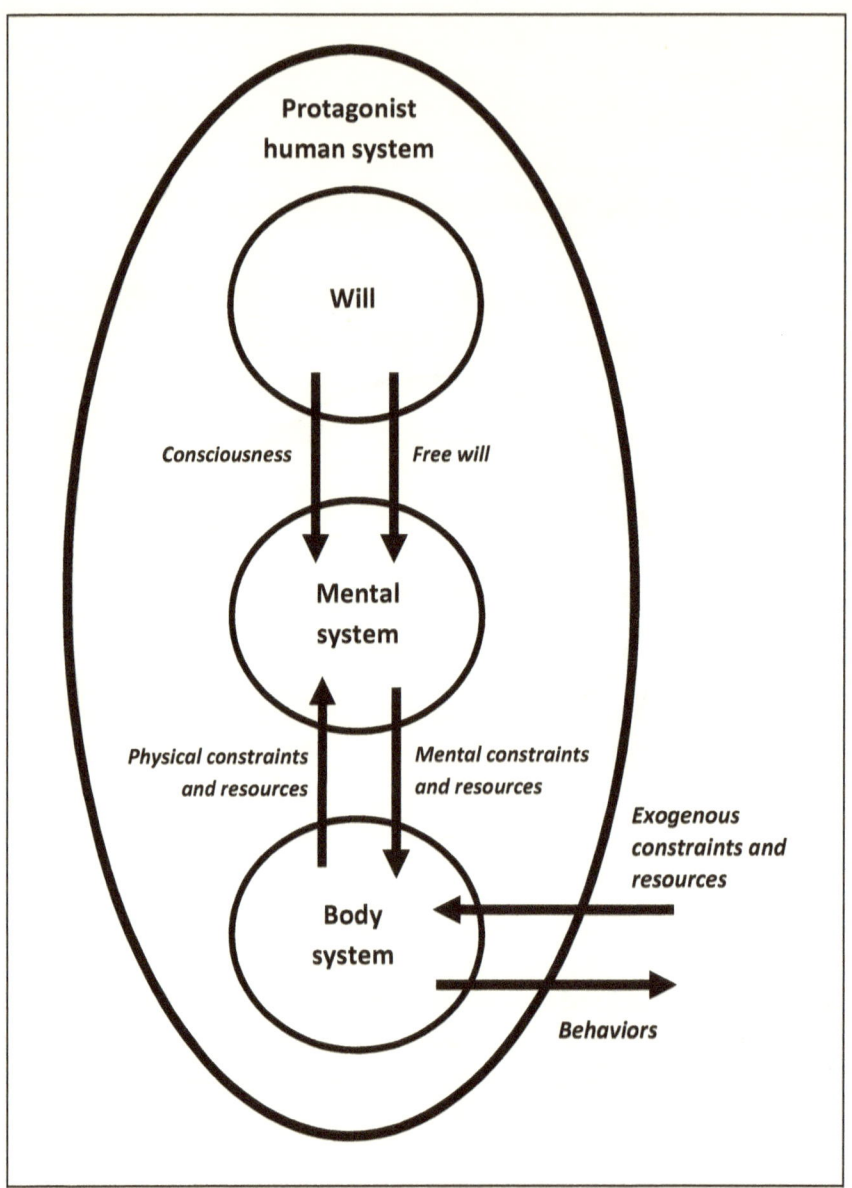

Figure 11: Global endogenous system.

In the group of the **exogenous systems** (which can be defined as the global exogenous system) we find the subsystems that constitute the human systems' external reality: the natural systems, the artificial systems, and the state systems.

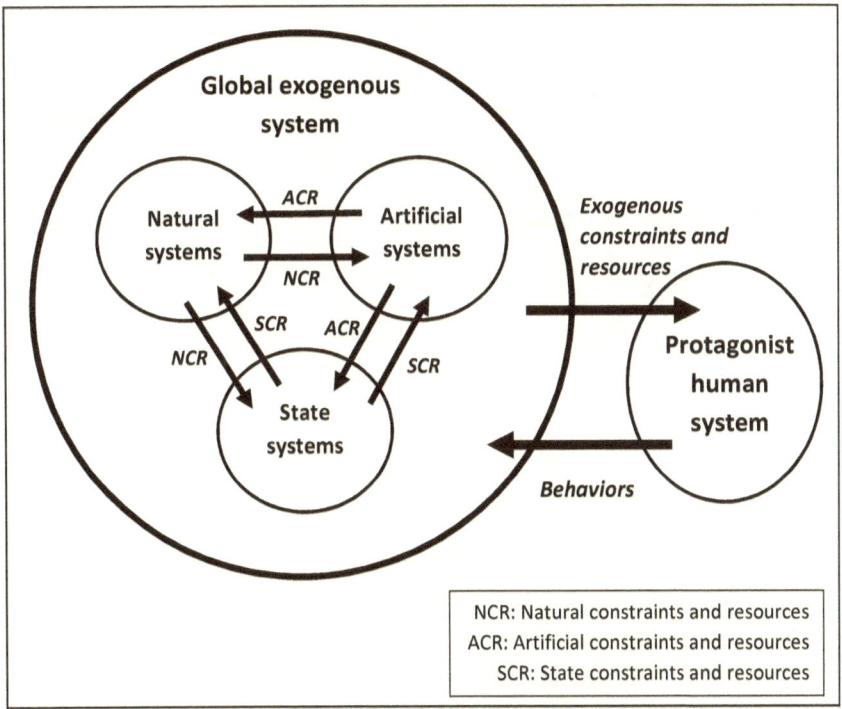

Figure 12: Global exogenous system.

The **natural systems**, also called ecological systems, are an entity that justifies its existence and functions as a whole through the interaction of the geographic, oceanic, climatic, and biological systems.

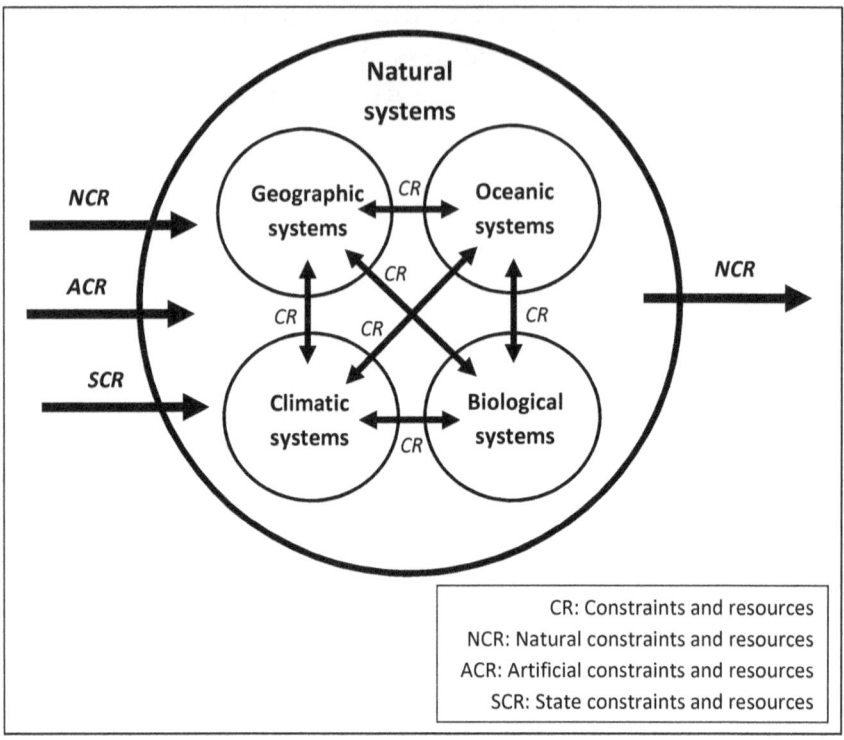

Figure 13: Natural systems.

The **artificial systems**, also called technological systems, are an entity that justifies its existence and functions as a whole through the interaction of the industrial systems and the educational systems. It is worth noting that technology is the set of knowledge and techniques that enable the development of certain industries and their related goods.

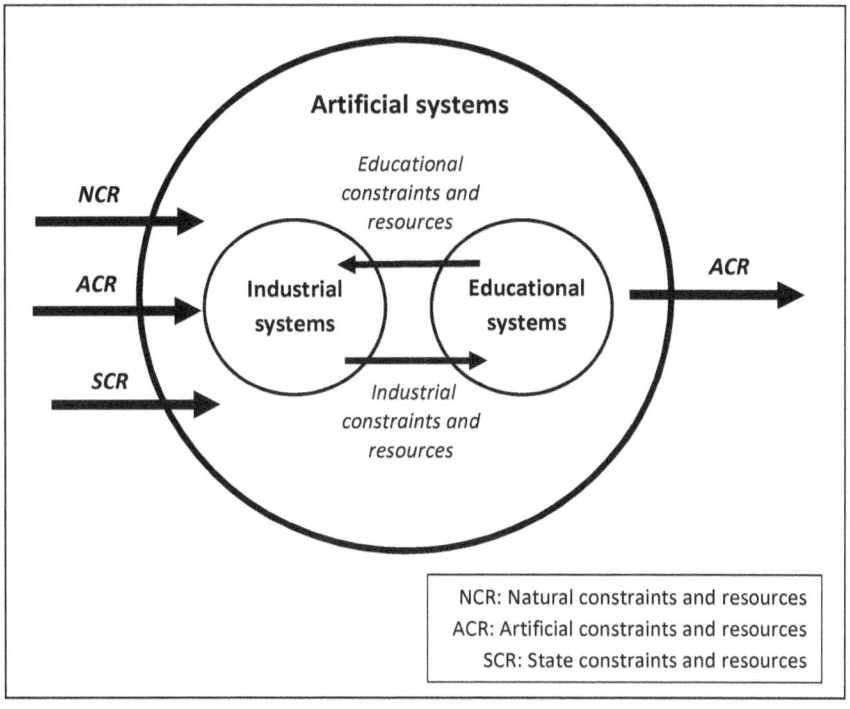

Figure 14: Artificial systems.

The **state systems** are an entity that justifies its existence and functions as a whole through the interaction of the political systems and the civil systems.

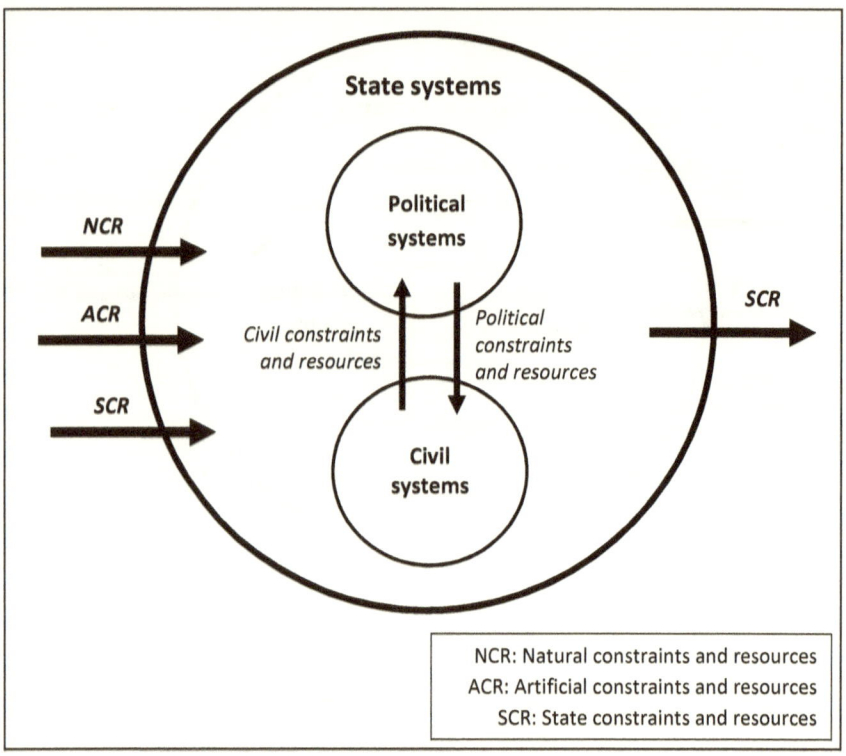

Figure 15: State systems.

The exogenous systems are all the systems that are part of the protagonist human system's environment and, therefore, are capable of affecting it.

For practical reasons, and in order to make it useful for the study of decision making, I have decided to group the different exogenous systems in three large subsystems: the artificial system, the natural system, and the state system.

The categorization of the different exogenous systems can be altered, depending on the case study; but for practical and didactic purposes, in this theory, these three large groups are representative of the three external realities that are constantly conditioning the human system in the decision making process.

This general classification of the exogenous systems that affect the protagonist corresponds with a global observation of reality.

In a particular case study, it may be more appropriate to present a singular expression of the exogenous systems that affect the protagonist. This particular classification would correspond with the study of the protagonist's closest environment; beyond the fact that the human system is a part of a global system that affects it.

The relevant question is: how do these exogenous systems affect the protagonist human system?

These three systems mentioned before affect the protagonist according to the interactions that they develop with it.

In order to evaluate these interactions, we must pay attention to the types of outputs they generate.

The natural system generates a set of natural constraints and resources, also called **natural factors**.

The artificial system generates a set of artificial constraints and resources, also called **artificial factors**.

The state system generates a set of state constraints and resources, also called **state factors**.

Their respective interactions with the protagonist will depend, in addition to their outputs, on how the three external systems relate to each other.

Moreover, the endogenous systems generate a set of spiritual, mental, and physical constraints and resources, called **spiritual, mental, and physical factors**, respectively.

In summary, the manifestation of the protagonist human system is a product of the interaction of its endogenous and exogenous factors, which define its particular way of life.

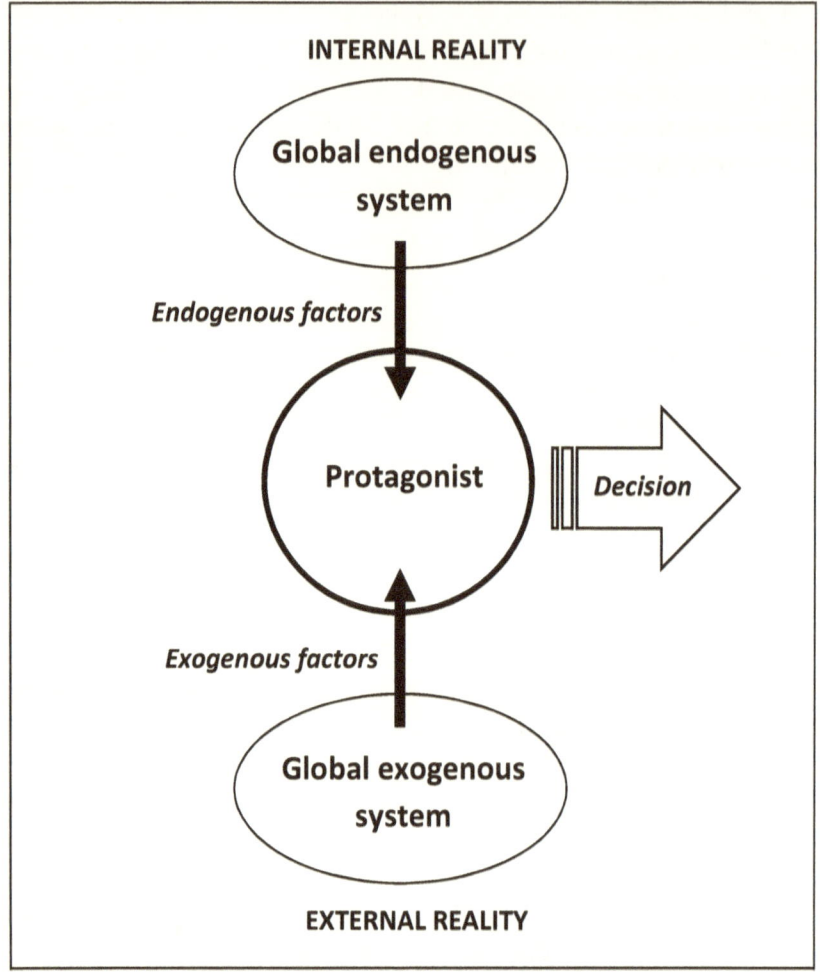

Figure 16: Way of life.

Way of life			
Exogenous factors		Endogenous factors	
Constraints	Resources	Constraints	Resources
Natural		Spiritual	
Artificial		Mental	
State		Physical	

Figure 17: Way of life.

Henceforth, when we talk about endogenous factors we will only pay attention to the mental and physical factors; since the mind is part of the soul, and the spiritual resources express themselves through the mind.

There is a current way of life and a desired way of life.

The **current way of life** is the set of endogenous and exogenous factors that define the human system's present lifestyle.

The **desired way of life** is the set of endogenous and exogenous factors that define the human system's desired lifestyle.

In general, human systems tend to make decisions that contribute to building, to a certain degree, the desired way of life.

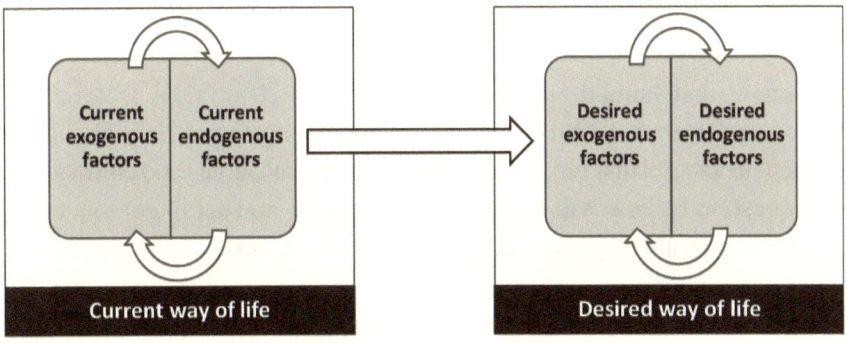

Figure 18: Current way of life and desired way of life.

THE DECISION SYSTEM

Decision is the act and effect of deciding.

Deciding is the mental action through which human systems determine their options of manifestation, which are restricted or enabled by certain endogenous and exogenous factors, and select the one they consider the most valuable according to their structure of preferences.

We know that human systems have mental and physical factors that represent certain internal resources and constraints, and they also have exogenous factors that represent certain external resources and constraints. The question is: how will human systems decide and act in consequence, given the internal and external circumstances that are affecting them?

There is a mental program that solves this question and provides a solution to all the decision needs that human systems face in their respective realities. This belief subsystem is called decision system.

The **decision system** is a belief subsystem that justifies its existence and functions as a whole through the interaction of the valuation system and the viability evaluation system. The input are sensory images (internal and external), and the output are decisions.

Decisions are projective thoughts that determine the future corporal actions that the human system will perform.

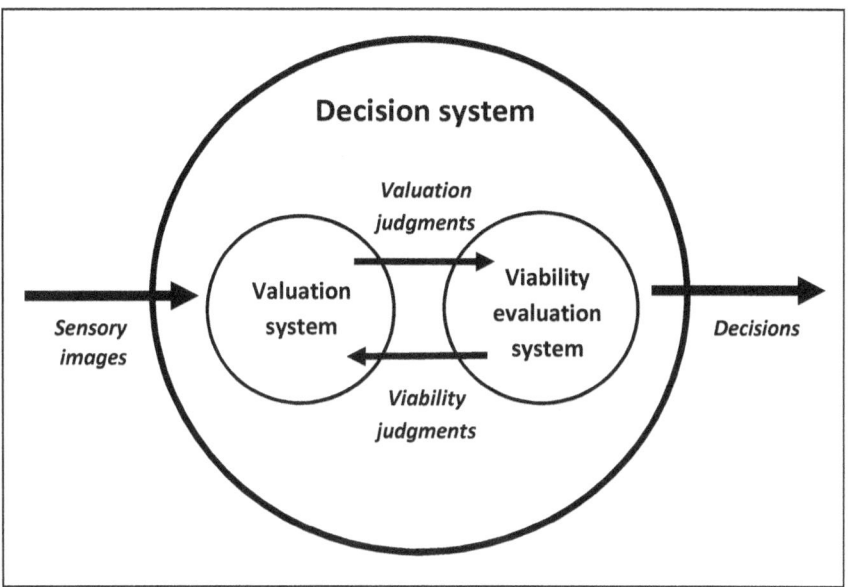

Figure 19: Decision system.

The **valuation system** is a belief subsystem that assigns a certain degree of relative value, positive or negative, to each element of the perceived reality.

When human systems contemplate their options of manifestation, their valuation system determines the relative value of each projected option. However, this is not enough to make the decision. In order to do that, the valuation system interacts with the viability evaluation system.

The **viability evaluation system** is a belief subsystem in charge of estimating the degree of viability or inviability of the contemplated options.

The **level of viability** is the degree of relative facileness to get the option evaluated by the human system. The **level of inviability** is the degree of relative difficulty to get the option evaluated by the human system.

In the following chapters, we will analyze the elements that compose the decision system, the laws that regulate their interrelations, and how they influence human behaviors.

The valuation system

All human systems have a **valuation system**. The valuation system is an active belief subsystem that turns sensory images into valuation thoughts.

Valuation thoughts manifest a valuation of different aspects of reality. They are also called valuation judgments.

To valuate is to assign a certain degree of relative value, positive or negative, to each element of the perceived reality.

The **value** is the degree of relative relevance, positive or negative, that the human system assigns to certain elements of reality.

The **relative relevance** is a certain amount of weighting that is altered according to the elements that are being compared and evaluated, subject to the criteria of a certain valuation system.

A valuation is the act and effect of valuating. **Valuations** are manifested through valuation judgments or valuation thoughts (they are synonyms), which are the emergent property of the valuation subsystem of the mental system.

The valuation thought may be positive or negative. If it is positive, it receives the name of **appreciative thought**. If it is negative, it can also be referred to as **derogatory thought**.

To illustrate these concepts, let us see the example of a person facing an external stimulus. That stimulus (that we will call Y1) enters his body system through the senses and is transmitted to the mental sensory system, which transforms it into a sensory image that later enters the belief system, and there, more specifically, gets in the valuation system.[6] Let us suppose that Y1 is a plate of food and, as a consequence, the mixed sensory image that enters the valuation system includes: the shape, the color, the taste, the smell, and the internal physical sensation of the first bite. When these images enter the valuation system, the latter emits a valuation thought (V1): "this meal is delicious." V1 is an appreciative thought, because it manifests a positive valuation of a certain aspect of reality (Y1).

Since V1 is a thought, we know that it has four elements: sensory images, linguistic meaning, energetic pole (in this case, it is positive), and a level of intensity, that corresponds with the amount of energy of the thought. By convention, we determine the intensity of thoughts on a scale from zero to ten. We may suppose that V1 has an intensity level of eight points, which is equal to the amount of weighting that the human system assigns to the stimulus Y1.

The same process can take place with internal mental stimuli; as, for example, the thought (Y2): "I have to get up early tomorrow." When Y2 enters the mental sensory system as a stimulus, this system decodes it and transmits it to the valuation system in the form of sensory images. Those invented images of the future, of himself making an effort to get up, are weighed by the person's valuation system, which emits the derogatory thought (V2): "I don't like getting up early," with an intensity level of six points. The intensity of six points is equivalent to the level of negative valuation held by V2.

The **valuation system** is an entity that justifies its existence and functions as a whole through the interaction of the internal valuation system and the external valuation system. The input of the valuation system are sensory images, and the output are valuation thoughts.

---

[6]   This process is illustrated in figure 1.

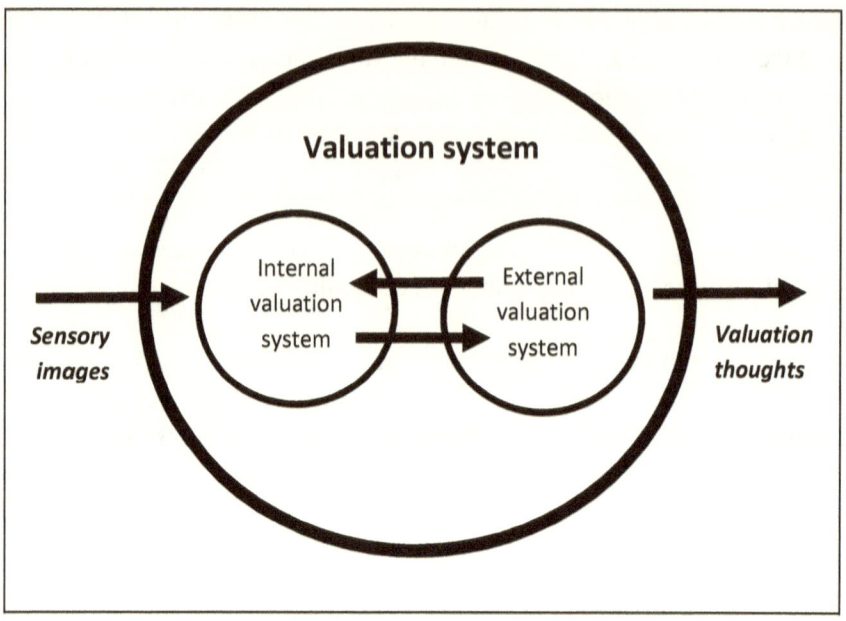

Figure 20: Valuation system.

The **internal valuation system** (or **self-valuation system**) is an entity that justifies its existence and functions as a whole through the interaction of the criteria of positive and negative self-valuation. The self-valuation system determines the mechanism by which the human system assigns valuations, positive or negative, to different aspects of its internal reality.

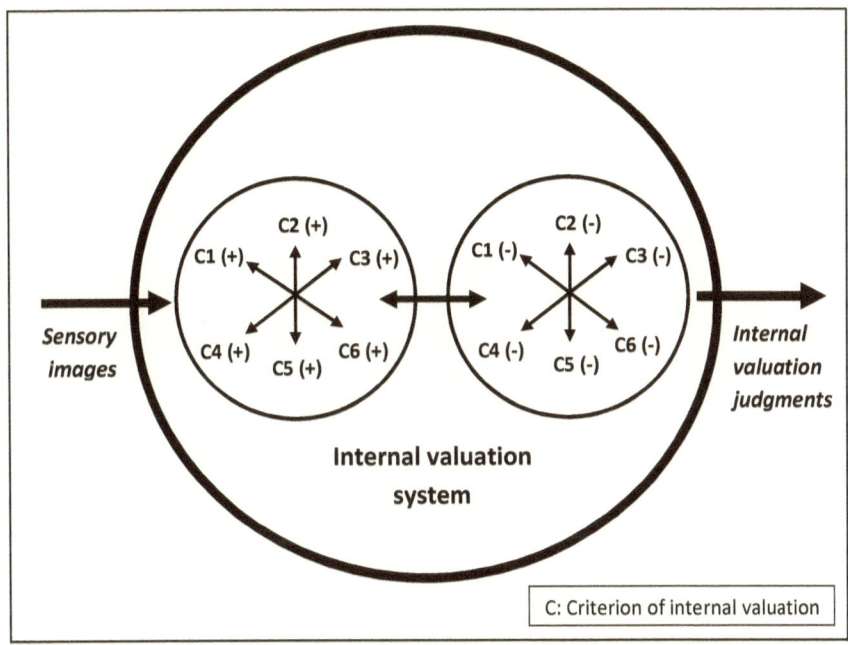

Figure 21: Internal valuation (self-valuation) subsystem.

The **external valuation system** is an entity that justifies its existence and functions as a whole through the interaction of the positive and negative criteria of external valuation. The external valuation system determines the mechanism by which the human system assigns valuations, positive or negative, to different aspects of its external reality.

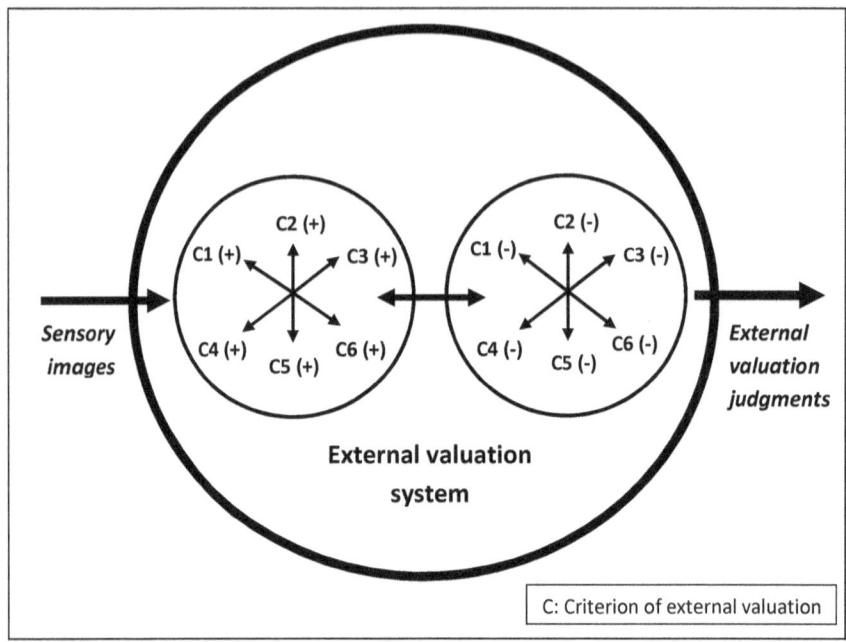

Figure 22: External valuation subsystem.

The **criteria of valuation** are associations of normative valuation beliefs that constitute the valuation subsystems and contribute to generating several valuation judgments about the different elements of reality that define the human system and its environment.

The criteria of valuation are a set of arguments that contribute to the validation, or not, to some degree, of all the factors of reality. The factors that are validated have a positive valuation, and the factors that are invalidated have a negative valuation. The factors of the environment are judged by the criteria of external valuation, and the factors of the internal reality are judged by the criteria of self-valuation.

For example, let us suppose that a person is standing in front of a mirror observing her own figure. When the visual sensory image of her body reflected on the mirror (stimulus Y) enters her belief system, it resonates with a set of criteria of valuation that may be summarized in the following way:

- Criteria of positive external valuation: "people who have an A body type are attractive," "society values the people who have an A body type," "fashion magazines always show people with an A body type."
- Criteria of negative external valuation: "people who have a B body type are not attractive," "society does not value the people who have a B body type," "the people with a B body type are mocked on TV."
- Criteria of positive self-valuation: "if I have an A body type, I am attractive," "if I am attractive, people appreciate me," "when people appreciate me, I value myself more."
- Criteria of negative self-valuation: "if I have a B body type, I am not attractive," "if I am not attractive, people look down on me," "when people look down on me, I value myself less."

From the interaction of these criteria, according to their energetic intensity and their level of resonance with the entering stimulus, an appreciative thought (V1) or a derogatory thought (V2) may emerge. In this case, V1 could be the thought: "I have an A body type, I am attractive, I approve my body," with a positive pole and an intensity level of seven points; and V2 could be the thought: "I have a B body type, I am not attractive, I disapprove my body," with a negative pole and an intensity level of eight points.

We may further summarize this example in the following way:

If Y=A, V1= +7

If Y=B, V2= −8

Where:

- Y is the stimulus
- A is the "A body type"
- B is the "B body type"
- V1 is the appreciative thought
- V2 is the derogatory thought
- The symbol + represents the positive pole

o   The symbol – represents the negative pole
o   The numbers represent the level of intensity, expressed in absolute values

The valuation level (positive or negative) of the thought will correspond with the intensity level (positive or negative, respectively) that it expresses.

The valuation system determines and constitutes the **valuation structure** (or "valuation hierarchy"), which is a structure of valuation judgments that are hierarchically organized according to the relative amount of weighting assigned to the different stimuli.

Let us see the example of a person who is at the office and imagines three possible activities for his next holidays. Those thoughts about the future are: "I could rest in a beach" (Y1), "I could stay at the office and finish the project that I'm working on" (Y2), and "I could stay at home and fix it up" (Y3). When these sensory images enter the valuation system, the latter emits, respectively, three valuation thoughts: "I enjoy resting in the beach" (V1), "I value finishing the project that I'm working on" (V2), and "I like living in a nice house" (V3). These appreciative thoughts have an intensity of nine, five, and two points, respectively. As a result, the valuation structure can be illustrated in the following way:

Valuation structure

	Valuation thoughts	Valuation level
V1	"I enjoy resting in the beach."	(+) 9
V2	"I value finishing the project that I'm working on."	(+) 5
V3	"I like living in a nice house."	(+) 2

Figure 23: Valuation structure. Example.

It should be noted that the valuation structure is mutable, since it is affected by each stimulus it receives and it varies according to the endogenous and exogenous factors that enable and restrict the protagonist human system that is performing the valuation.

Types of valuations

Valuations may be analyzed according to different categories, some of which will be mentioned in this chapter.[7]

Positive valuation: The human system manifests a positive valuation thought about a certain phenomenon of reality.

Negative valuation: The human system manifests a negative valuation thought about a certain phenomenon of reality.

Conscious valuation: The human system manifests a valuation thought about a certain phenomenon and is aware of it.

Unconscious valuation: The human system manifests a valuation thought about a certain phenomenon without being aware of it.

Strong valuation: The human system manifests a valuation thought of a relatively high intensity about a certain phenomenon of reality.

Moderate valuation: The human system manifests a valuation thought of a relatively moderate intensity about a certain phenomenon of reality.

Weak valuation: The human system manifests a valuation thought of a relatively low intensity about a certain phenomenon of reality.

---

[7] The different typologies that will be named throughout the book do not necessarily constitute a complete list.

Internal valuation: The human system manifests a valuation thought about a phenomenon of the internal reality. Any kind of internal valuation is also called self-valuation.

External valuation: The human system manifests a valuation thought about a phenomenon of the external reality.

Corporal self-valuation: The human system manifests a valuation thought about a phenomenon related to its body system.

Mental self-valuation: The human system manifests a valuation thought about a phenomenon related to its mental system.

Physical external valuation: The human system manifests a valuation thought about a phenomenon of its physical environment.

Human external valuation: The human system manifests a valuation thought about an external human system.

Corporal external valuation: The human system manifests a valuation thought about the state of an external human system's body.

Mental external valuation: The human system manifests a valuation thought about the mental state of an external human system.

Individual external valuation: The human system manifests a valuation thought about an individual human system.

Social external valuation: The human system manifests a valuation thought about a social system.

Individual valuation: An individual human system manifests a valuation thought about some aspect of reality.

Social valuation: A social system manifests a valuation thought about some aspect of reality.

Dependent self-valuation: The human system needs to obtain certain types of capital and experience certain situations in order to be able to nourish its own self-esteem.[8]

Independent self-valuation: The human system does not need to obtain certain types capital and does not need to experience certain situations in order to be able to nourish its own self-esteem.

Influenceable external valuation: The human system is influenced by certain agents in its external valuation of certain phenomena.

Influenceable self-valuation: The human system is influenced by certain agents in its self-valuation.

Autonomous self-valuation: The human system does not let itself be influenced by any external agent to emit a valuation thought about its own characteristics.

Autonomous external valuation: The human system does not let itself to be influenced by any external agent to generate a valuation thought about a certain external phenomenon.

Superior self-valuation: The human system manifests a superior self-valuation compared to one or more competing human systems.

Inferior self-valuation: The human system manifests an inferior self-valuation compared to one or more competing human systems.

Competitive self-valuation: The human system competes with one or more human systems in order to determine its own self-esteem. The competition is based on a comparative evaluation of one or several factors that the human systems share in different gradations.

It is worth noting that all the types of valuations that a human system can generate are based on a comparative evaluation (due to the relativity of the valuation phenomenon).

---

[8] This subject will be explained in detail in the chapter "The need for self-esteem and its satisfaction mechanisms."

Furthermore, the weightings are not absolute, but rather they have different levels. They weight certain aspects of reality and follow the different criteria of valuation by which the human system develops different valuation judgments.

Finally, it is important to clarify that the categories can be combined, to be able to explain with more precision a certain valuation phenomenon. For example, we may speak of a "strong, positive external valuation."

Laws of well-being and valuation

According to the **law of the emotional well-being maximization**, all human systems seek to maximize their emotional well-being.

According to the **law of the emotional ill-being minimization**, all human systems seek to minimize their emotional ill-being.

This means that between two or more options that human systems consider viable, they will always choose the one that maximizes they emotional well-being or the one that minimizes their ill-being (if the option of well-being is not available).

According to the **law of well-being**, there is a directly proportional causal relationship between the relative degree of approval that an emergent thought manifests and the relative degree of emotional well-being that the human system experiences. The higher the degree of approval that a thought expresses, the higher the equivalent degree of well-being that it generates. The lower the degree of approval that a thought expresses, the lower the equivalent degree of well-being that it generates.

The **law of ill-being** determines that there is a directly proportional causal relationship between the relative degree of rejection that an emergent thought manifests and the relative degree of emotional ill-being that the human system experiences. The higher the degree of rejection that a thought expresses, the higher the equivalent degree of ill-being that it generates. The lower the degree of rejection that a thought expresses, the lower the equivalent degree of ill-being that it generates.

The **law of positive valuation** establishes that there is a directly proportional causal relationship between the relative degree of emotional well-being that a thought generates and the relative degree of positive valuation that the human system assigns to it. The higher the degree of emotional well-being that a thought generates, the higher the equivalent degree of positive valuation that the human system assigns to it. The lower the degree of emotional well-being that a thought generates, the lower the equivalent degree of positive valuation that the human system assigns to it.

The **law of negative valuation** determines that there is a directly proportional causal relationship between the relative degree of emotional ill-being that a thought generates and the relative degree of negative valuation that the human system assigns to it. The higher the degree of emotional ill-being that a thought generates, the higher the equivalent degree of negative valuation that the human system assigns to it. The lower the degree of emotional ill-being that a thought generates, the lower the equivalent degree of negative valuation that the human system assigns to it.

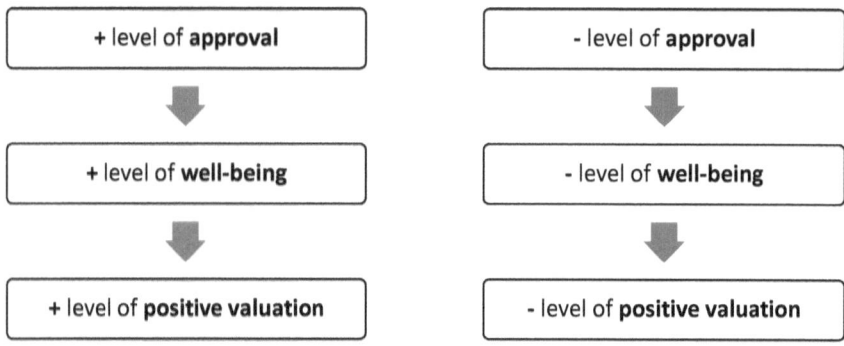

Figure 24: Laws of well-being and positive valuation.

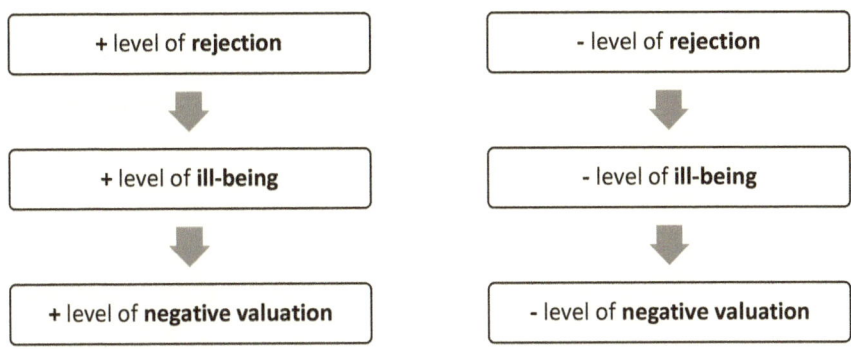

Figure 25: Laws of ill-being and negative valuation.

To illustrate these laws, let us go back to the example of figure 23. We know that, in this person's valuation structure, V1 ("I enjoy resting in the beach") has a positive valuation of nine points, V2 ("I value finishing the project that I'm working on") has a positive valuation of five points, and V3 ("I like living in a nice house") has a positive valuation of two points. We can infer, according to the laws of well-being and positive valuation, that V1 generates a level of well-being of nine points, V2 five points, and V3 two points; as a consequence of having a level of approval of nine, five, and two points, respectively.

Following the law of the emotional well-being maximization, we know that this human system will choose option V1 and will decide to act accordingly, because V1 is the viable option that he considers will provide the highest level of well-being.

Let us see another example in which a person has two derogatory thoughts in her valuation structure: "I don't like going to work" (W1), with a negative valuation of grade four; and "I couldn't stand being unemployed" (W2), with a degree of negative valuation of eight points. The law of negative valuation tells us that W1 generates in this person a level of ill-being of four points, as a consequence a level four of rejection, and that W2 generates in her a level of ill-being of eight points, as a consequence a level eight of rejection.

In addition, due to the law of the emotional ill-being minimization, we know that if this human system does not see another option, between the factor weighted in W1 ("going to work") and the factor weighted in W2 ("being unemployed") she will choose the option that generates the lowest level of ill-being. That option is the one expressed in W1, because it has the lowest level of negative valuation; in other words, this person will choose to go to work.

From the laws mentioned above, we can deduce the **law of selective criterion**: the human system will choose to materialize the thoughts about the future that are relatively more valued.

That is to say, the human system will choose to materialize the projected option that has a higher level of positive valuation, or a lower level of negative valuation (in the case in which no options with positive valuations are available).

In the examples mentioned in this chapter, the first person will decide to materialize the weighted option that has the highest level of positive valuation (V1), and the second person will choose the projected option that has the lowest level of negative valuation (W1).

Along with the law of selective criterion, we can infer another principle from the postulates stated in this chapter: the **law of the valuation magnitude**. This law establishes that the level of positive valuation of a thought is equivalent to the level of approval it manifests; also, the level of negative valuation of a thought is equivalent to the level of rejection it manifests.

Finally, the law of **relative valuation** states that all the subjective values that the human system assigns to the different options of reality are due to an act of comparison with other elements of reality.

In order to assign values to the different options, the human system needs to perform a comparative evaluation. The assigned weightings depend, among other variables, on the type and number of compared options.

In conclusion, **there is no valuation without comparison**. For this reason, the amount of weighting of an option of reality is assigned in relation to other options that are contemplated in the act of comparative evaluation.

This implies that the levels of approval and rejection, and the levels of well-being and ill-being, are relative too.

The assigned valuations that we have seen in the examples could change if the human system added new options to its valuation structure.

For the first example, we could think that if the person contemplated the option of "taking a year off to travel around the world," the valuation of "resting in the beach" would be lower, in comparison with the new thought that he had not contemplated before.

In the second example, if the human system contemplated a work option that caused her a very high level of rejection, the valuation of her current job would increase (that is to say, the person would value her current job more, compared to a much worse job).

Phases in the gestation of rational behaviors

According to the **law of rational behavior**, all rational human systems develop a series of organized behaviors that fulfill a specific plan in order to serve an end, which consists in satisfying a certain need that is superior to others in value, in certain circumstances.

There are different **phases in the gestation of rational behaviors**, which may be summarized in the following way: the valuation system determines a valuation structure, which in turn determines and constitutes the structure of needs, which determines and constitutes the structure of ends. The human system, subsequently, makes a plan for achieving the most valuable ends and proceeds to execute the sequence of planned behaviors. The results are the interaction of behaviors and reality. The human system expects that the results will be the attainment of the ends that will allow it to satisfy those needs that have a higher level of valuation (see figure 26).

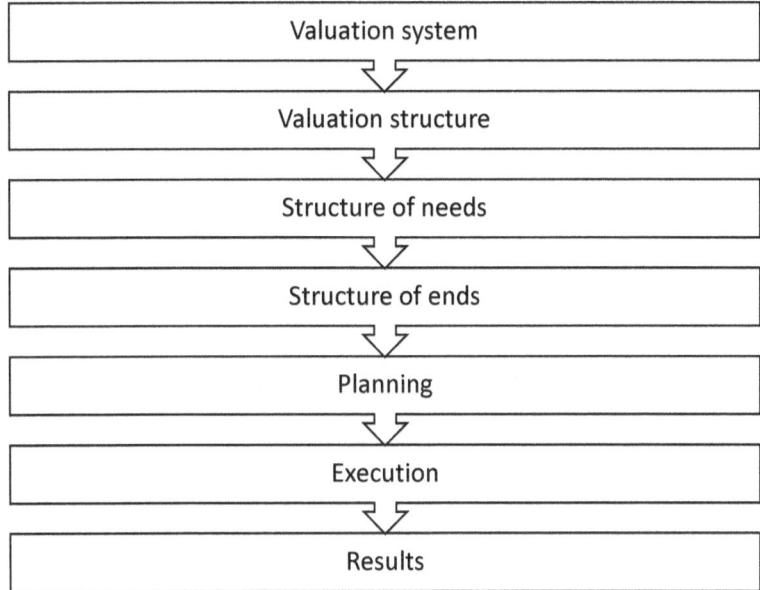

Figure 26: Phases in the gestation and execution of rational behaviors.

As we know, to valuate is to assign a certain degree of value, positive or negative, to a certain element of reality.

The **valuation system** is the belief subsystem in charge of valuating all the stimuli that the mental system receives.

The valuation is the act and effect of valuating. All weightings are relative, and they are manifested through valuation judgments (also called "valuation thoughts"), which are the emergent property of the valuation system.

The valuation system determines and constitutes the valuation structure (or "valuation hierarchy"), which is a structure of weighting judgments.

It should be remembered that the valuation structure is mutable, since it is affected by each stimulus it receives and it varies according to the endogenous and exogenous factors that enable and restrict the protagonist human system that is valuating.

Needs are what the human system lacks of and wishes to satisfy. We need something that we value but we do not have. This means that there is not a necessity without a previous valuation judgment about something one wants to obtain. The recognition of the absence, and therefore of the need, responds to a previous exercise of valuation that determined the positive value of a phenomenon (a desired experience, object, or service) that the person does not possess.

To prefer is to assign more weight to an option, compared with another or others. The preferred, most valued option is the chosen one. To choose is to select an option of manifestation among several ones.

The valuation structure determines and constitutes the **structure of needs**, which is a structure of judgments of necessity that are hierarchically organized according to the relative amount of weighting assigned to them.

The needs that the human system wishes to satisfy become ends that the person seeks to achieve. There is a hierarchy of needs based on the different valuations that are assigned to them (which are expressed in the hierarchy of valuations). In addition, there is a hierarchy of ends that depends on the hierarchy of needs.

The structure of needs determines and constitutes the **structure of ends**. The latter represents a structure of teleological judgments that are hierarchically organized according to the relative valuations that have been assigned to them.

All ends serve certain needs. There are multiple needs and, therefore, multiple ends that the human system seeks to achieve. The multiplicity of needs and ends leads to the gestation of the structures of needs and ends, where the second one depends on the first one.

In summary, the procedure described until now would be the following: the human system performs a process of valuation that recognizes the existence of a need it wishes to satisfy, and then it turns that need into a certain end to achieve. The objective that the human system wants to attain may possibly be accomplished through various means.

The human system emits a series of projective thoughts about the means that are necessary to achieve the end. The different means are weighted, and the preferred ones are chosen. This is the **planning** phase.

Ultimately, the valuation system determines the structure of valuations, needs, ends, and means to reach those ends. Valuation judgments can be made about all types of options. In fact, **valuation judgments are made at all the levels of the decision making process**.

Once the planning is done, the human systems proceeds to execute the sequence of planned behaviors. This constitutes the **execution** phase.

The execution of those behaviors will cause a series of changes in reality, defined as **results**. The human system will try to achieve those results that express the attainment of the ends desired in this sequence.

In figure 27, this process is illustrated by an example.

A person is working at the office and realizes that soon he will be able to take some days off.

His **valuation system** generates the following valuation structure:

Valuation structure

	Valuation thoughts	Valuation level
V1	"I enjoy resting in the beach."	(+) 9
V2	"I value finishing the project that I'm working on."	(+) 5
V3	"I like living in a nice house."	(+) 2

Structure of needs

	Judgments of necessity	Hierarchic order
N1	"I need to rest in the beach."	1
N2	"I need to finish the project that I'm working on."	2
N3	"I need to live in a nice house."	3

Structure of ends

	Teleological judgments	Hierarchic order
E1	"I'm going to take some days off and travel to the beach."	1
E2	"I'm going to stay at the office and finish the project."	2
E3	"I'm going to take some days off and fix my house."	3

The most valued option is chosen: **E1**

Planning

Projective thoughts
"I'm going to talk to my boss to ask for some days off."
"This weekend, I'm going to search for possible destinations and choose one."
"Next week, I'm going to a travel agency to make all the reservations."

Execution

The series of planned behaviors is executed.

Results

Some weeks later, the person is sitting at the beach.

Figure 27: Phases in the gestation and execution
of rational behaviors. Example.

In figure 27, we have seen the case of a valuation hierarchy with a positive charge. In this example, since all the judgments are positive, the human system chooses the option that has the highest level of positive valuation and acts accordingly.

But the structure could also include negative valuations. In that case, the negative weightings would be placed under the positive ones in the hierarchic order.

If the valuation structure had only negative valuation judgments, given certain circumstances, the human system would choose the negative option with the lowest level of intensity.

Let us see a situation in which a person is pondering what to do during the rest of his day, and the only viable options are:

1- "Taking care of my sick mother."
2- "Staying home to rest."

Option n°1 causes him a degree of ill-being of three points, because it makes him sad to see his mother suffering. Option n°2 causes him a degree of ill-being of eight points; which is the level of intensity of the emotion of guilt he would suffer staying at home, knowing that his mother is ill.

In figure 28, we can see this human system's valuation hierarchy and how it translates into a hierarchy of needs and ends, until it reaches the phases of planning, execution, and results.

Valuation structure

	Valuation thoughts	Valuation level
V1	"I don't like taking care of my sick mother."	(-) 3
V2	"It is unacceptable to stay at home when my mother needs me."	(-) 8

Structure of needs

	Judgments of necessity	Hierarchic order
N1	"I need to take care of my sick mother."	1
N2	"I need to stay at home and rest."	2

Structure of ends

	Teleological judgments	Hierarchic order
E1	"I'm going to take care of my sick mother."	1
E2	"I'm going to stay at home and rest."	2

The option with the lowest level of negative valuation is chosen: **E1**

Planning

Projective thoughts
"I'm going to call my mother to let her know I'm going to her house."
"I'm going to take the car out of the garage."
"I'm going to drive to my mother's home."

Execution

The series of planned behaviors is executed.

Results

The person is at his mother's house, taking care of her.

Figure 28: Phases in the gestation and execution
of rational behaviors. Example.

Until now, we have seen two simple examples, in which we suppose there is only one end for each need, and there are three means that the human system needs to execute to satisfy that end. However, needs may have several levels of complexity.

The complexity of the need depends on the number of sub-needs, ends, and means that must be attained in order to satisfy it.

According to the **law of complexity of the need**, the level of complexity of a necessity is directly proportional to the number of sub-needs, ends, and means that must be attained in order to satisfy it. The higher the level of complexity of a need, the higher the number of sub-needs, ends, and means that must be attained to satisfy it. The lower the level of complexity of a need, the lower the number of sub-needs, ends, and means that must be attained to satisfy it.

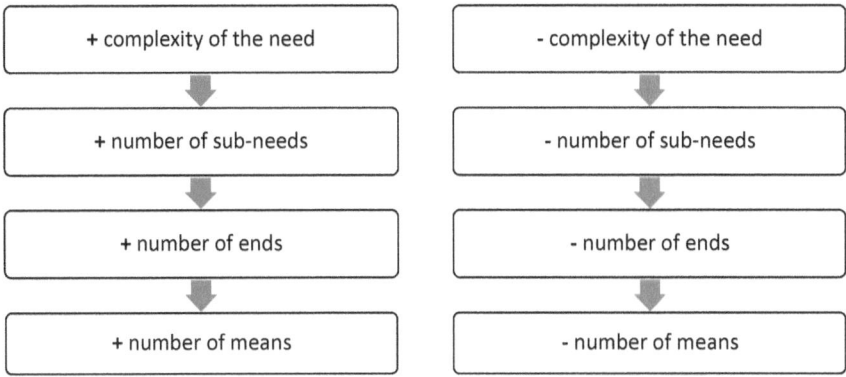

Figure 29: Law of complexity of the need.

There are very simple needs, like the ones that do not have sub-needs and are satisfied with only one end and one means. For example: "I'm thirsty, I need water" (Nx), "I'm going to drink water" (Ex), "I'm going to grab a glass of water and drink it" (Mx).

Nx ———▶ **Ex** ———▶ **Mx**

Figure 30: Diagram of a simple need. Example.

There are also needs with a high level of complexity, which require a great number of sub-needs, ends, and means that must be attained in order to satisfy it. An example of this case would be: "I need a college degree" (superior need Ny), that implies the sub-needs: "I need money to pay for college" (sub-need N_1) and "I need to pass thirty two courses" (sub-needs N_2-N_{33}). The structure of ends includes: "I'm going to look for a job to pay for college" (E_1), "I'm going to attend all the classes and study for each exam" (E_2-E_{33}); and the structure of means includes: "I'm going to write my resume" (M_1), "I'm going to read job ads" (M_2), "I'm going to submit my college application" (M_3), "I'm going to buy the reading materials" (M_4), among others.

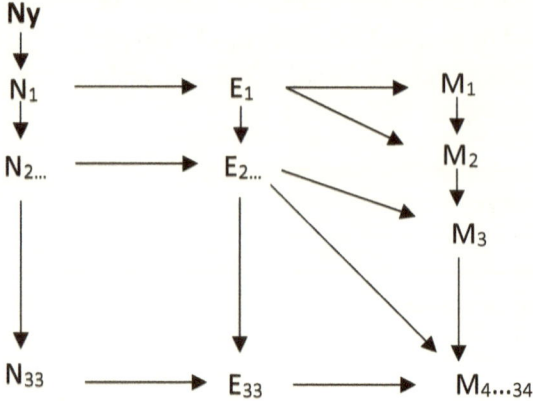

Figure 31: Diagram of a complex need. Example.

Simple needs require a relatively low number of actions and decisions for their satisfaction. Complex needs require a relatively high number of actions and decisions for their satisfaction.

This is what the **law of complexity of the decision diagram** expresses: the more complex the need is, the higher the number of decisions and actions required for its satisfaction. In other words, the higher the level of complexity of the need, the higher the level of complexity of the decision diagram; and the lower the level of complexity of the need, the lower the level of complexity of the decision diagram.

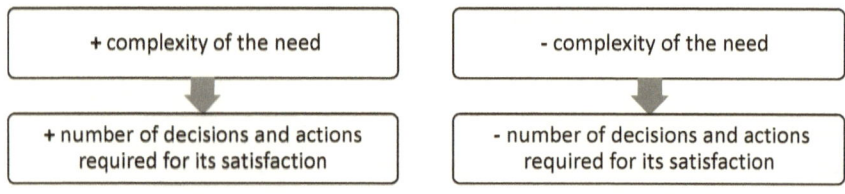

Figure 32: Law of complexity of the decision diagram.

The need for self-esteem and its satisfaction mechanisms

Self-esteem is the act and effect of assigning oneself a certain degree of positive valuation. To esteem is to appreciate, or to positively value, a certain phenomenon.

According to the **law of self-valuation**, there is a directly proportional causal relationship between the level of self-approval that human systems manifest toward themselves and the level of positive self-valuation they experience. On the other hand, there is a directly proportional causal relationship between the level of self-rejection that human systems manifest toward themselves and the level of negative self-valuation they experience.

In other words, positive self-referential thoughts contribute to increasing the human system's level of self-esteem, and negative self-referential thoughts contribute to lowering the level of self-esteem of the human system who emits them.

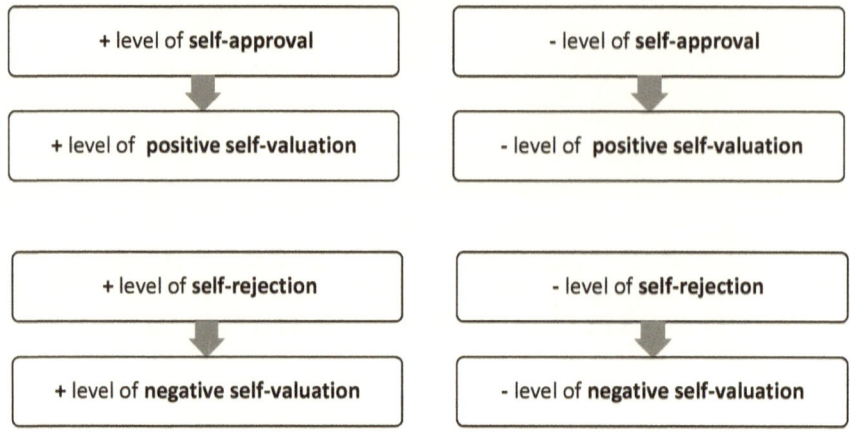

Figure 33: Law of self-valuation.

In general, in order to satisfy the need for positive self-valuation, human systems seek to attain other needs, which constitute the ends to satisfy their particular **self-esteem equation**.

All human systems need to valuate themselves positively. And all human systems seek to satisfy that need. However, the mechanisms of satisfaction depend on each person's particular valuation system.

Specifically, the subsystem of self-valuation is the one that determines the set of programs that the human system will follow in order to achieve the satisfaction of the need for self-esteem. The understanding of this programs enables the comprehension of the multiple needs and ends that the human system will pursue in order to attain the necessity of positive self-valuation.

From what has been said, we can deduce that the need for positive self-valuation permanently generates multiple needs. This is the case of a human system whose need for self-esteem is dependent. The phenomenon of **valuation dependency** is representative of the vast majority of human systems.

There are very few human systems whose needs for self-esteem are satisfied through self-sufficient psychological mechanisms. This would imply the existence of a particular structure of valuation beliefs that enabled the human system to self-assign itself a positive value and to keep it without needing to obtain anything external. It would be a state of positive self-valuation generated by a mechanism of unconditional self-approval.

This mechanism tends to be extremely difficult to find in a human system in an innate manner. However, in some cases, the belief structure may reform itself to enable this type of mechanism of independent self-valuation.

Returning to reality, a situation of independent self-valuation is very rare and special, and it is not representative of the general self-valuation mechanisms of the human race.

In summary, the human systems' dependent self-valuation is a defining variable of the collective personality of the global social system; and, for that reason, it is of great value to study and understand the diverse factors of valuation dependency.

Factors of valuation dependency

The human systems that have a mechanism of dependent self-valuation need to accumulate certain types of capital that, according to their particular criterion of self-valuation, are the means that allow them to preserve and increase their self-esteem.

Capital is a beneficial factor of reality that, when accumulated, increases the level of self-esteem of the entity that possesses it. When it is obtained and incremented, capital is a factor that is positively valued by the human system and contributes to increasing the person's self-esteem.

In the next pages, we will mention different types of capital that (individual or collective) human systems want to obtain and accumulate.

Social capital refers to the relative relevance and size of the social network that a human system possesses, and that person's affiliation to different types of social systems.

Economic capital refers to the relative amount of monetary, material, and financial capital that a human system owns.

Monetary capital refers to the relative amount of money and purchasing power that a human system has.

Material capital refers to the relative amount and the type of material goods that a human system owns.

Financial capital refers to the relative amount and the type of financial assets that a human system owns.

Dietary capital refers to the different substances that a certain human system regularly ingests to nurture its body system.

Health capital refers to the relative level of functional harmony that the mental system and the body system of a certain person manifest.

Mental health capital refers to the relative level of functional harmony that a certain person's mental system manifests.

Corporal health capital refers to the relative level of functional harmony that a certain person's body system manifests.

Political capital refers to the relative number and types of followers, from the civil system and the political system, that a human system can get to impose its will on public affairs.

Intellectual capital refers to the relative level of development of the different intellectual capacities.

Educational capital refers to the relative level of training achieved in the formal educational system.

Cultural capital refers to the relative degree of erudition that a human systems possesses.

Spiritual capital (or ethical capital) refers to the relative level of development of the virtues that a human system possesses.

Human capital refers to the relative level of development of the human system's corporal, intellectual, and spiritual capacities. In other words, the human capital includes the corporal, intellectual, and spiritual capital that constitute the human system.[9]

Aesthetic capital refers to the degree of relative beauty that a human system manifests. The aesthetic capital may be divided into corporal aesthetic capital and material aesthetic capital.

Corporal aesthetic capital refers to the degree of relative beauty that a certain person's body system manifests.

Material aesthetic capital refers to the degree of relative beauty that a certain type of material capital manifests (for example, clothing, house decoration, and automobiles).

Professional capital refers to the professional role that a human system plays and the relative level of work performance it manifests.

External professional capital refers to a certain type of professional service that a human system employs or consumes.

Physical capital refers to the relative level of development of the physical capacities that a human system has.

Affective capital refers to the relative level of positive affection that a human system obtains from one or more human systems. Affective capital includes the phenomena of individual and collective external approval.

Individual affective capital refers to the relative level of positive affection that a human system obtains from an individual. It comprises the phenomenon of individual external approval.

---

[9]   We will expand on the subjects of physical, intellectual, and spiritual capacities in the book *Educational Systems Theory. A model based on Mental and Social Systems* (see the section "Related works" at the end of this book).

Social affective capital refers to the relative level of positive affection that a human system obtains from a social system. It comprises the phenomenon of collective external approval.

Emotional capital is the relative degree of recurrence and level of emotional well-being that a human system experiences.

The types of capital mentioned before are only some of the many factors that human systems positively value.

It is worth noting that the capital assessment is done in relative terms. Moreover, its positive valuation depends on the particular personality of each human system. This means that some human systems positively value factors that perhaps other human systems value negatively.

Capital is accumulated according to a particular mechanism of dependent, positive self-valuation, which can be expressed by the self-esteem equation.

The self-esteem equation

In order to satisfy the need for self-esteem, the human system must attain other needs that constitute the means to successfully fulfill the former.

In simple words, the need for self-esteem is satisfied by attaining other needs. That is to say, the need for self-esteem is subordinated to the satisfaction of other necessities and ends.[10]

The sequence of the desired phenomena that are necessary to reach the end of positive self-valuation is expressed by the self-esteem equation. This equation is an algorithm that determines the order of the needs and ends that the human system wishes to attain in order to preserve or increase its level of self-esteem.

---

[10]   It should be pointed out that the self-esteem equation only makes reference to the humans systems that have a dependent self-valuation mechanism.

Let us remember that the concept of **self-esteem** is used as a synonym for positive self-valuation. The equation will dictate what kind of phenomena and/or capital the person wants to obtain and accumulate to preserve and increase its positive self-valuation.

The **self-esteem equation** is a set of associated criteria of valuation that determine the hierarchy of valuations, needs, and ends which guide human behavior to preserve and increase the human system's self-esteem.

The higher the level of satisfaction of the self-esteem equation is, the higher the level of positive self-valuation the human system will experience; and the lower the level of satisfaction of the self-esteem equation is, the lower the level of positive self-valuation will be.

On the contrary, the higher the level of dissatisfaction of the self-esteem equation, the higher the level of negative self-valuation; and the lower the level of dissatisfaction of the self-esteem equation, the lower the level of negative self-valuation.

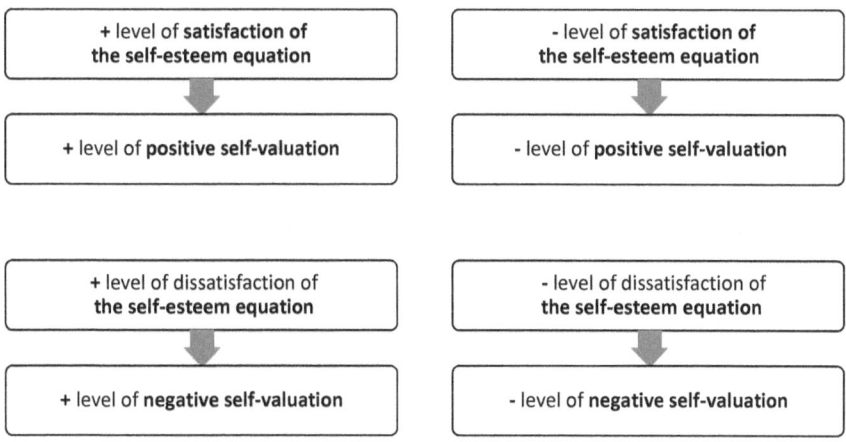

Figure 34: Correlations between the self-esteem equation and self-valuation.

The self-esteem equation determines the order of the phenomena that the human system wants to experience in order to get its own self-approval and, therefore, its positive self-valuation.

All human systems seek to maximize the level of their personal well-being and, for that reason, they seek to maximize the level of self-acceptance.

The fundamental difference lies in the fact that human systems, because of their particular active belief systems, have different valuation systems and structures of needs, which direct the pursuit of self-acceptance through different roads.

Not all of us want the same. Even though there are similarities, the distinctions among valuation criteria determine the existence of different self-esteem equations for each human system.

The diverse self-esteem equations are expressed by different value correlations.

Value correlations

Value correlations are a programed sequence of causes and effects that contribute to the satisfaction of a certain human system's self-esteem equation.

The correlations differ according to **four variables involved in the self-esteem equation**: the amount of capital, the types of capital, the relations of dependence between the different types of capital, and the diversity of capital.

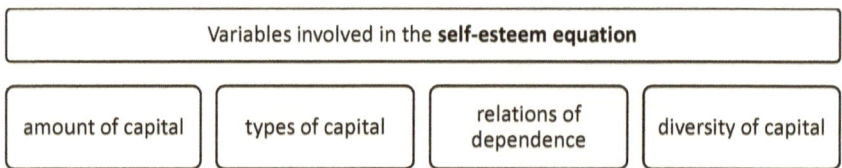

Figure 35: Variables of the self-esteem equation.

The **amount of capital** refers to the level of development that the desired capital must reach in order to satisfy the self-esteem equation. The higher the amount of desired capital that is obtained, the higher the level of satisfaction of the self-esteem equation.

The **types of capital** are the different positive factors that the human system seeks to obtain and accumulate in order to satisfy its self-esteem equation. The lower the level of complexity of the desired capital, the easier the satisfaction of the self-esteem equation.

The **relations of dependence** refer to the order of subordination that exists between the various types of capital that constitute the self-esteem equation.

The **diversity of capital** refers to the quantity of factors involved in the self-esteem equation that are positively valued and desired. The lower the diversity of the capital involved in the self-valuation equation, the easier the satisfaction of the equation.

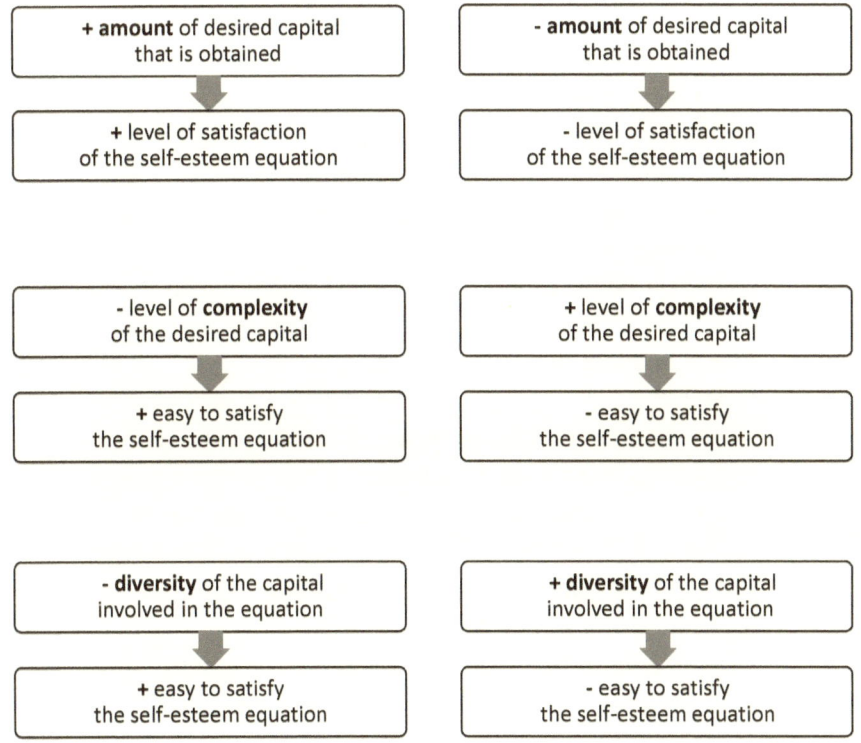

Figure 36: Correlations between the variables and the self-esteem equation.

The influence of self-valuation has two possible outcomes: a certain level of positive self-valuation, or a certain level of negative self-valuation.

The correlations can be expressed by identifying the types of capital involved in the equation or by employing certain phenomenic categories that substitute the concept of capital. Depending on the case, some categories are more useful than others for the explanation.

Let us see some examples of value correlations:

Correlation 1:

A. The human system X acquires a loan.
B. With that loan, X buys a certain automobile.
C. X gives the automobile to his wife, as a present.
D. X's wife feels very happy with the present and manifests a deep affection (approval) for X.
E. Due to the high level of positive affection and approval that his wife has expressed to him, X approves himself in the same proportion.
F. By experiencing the phenomenon E, X increases his self-esteem.

Now, we will express the same correlation using the concept of capital:

A. The human system X acquires a certain type of monetary capital (C1).
B. X uses C1 to buy a certain type of material capital (C2).
C. X gives C2 to his wife, as a present.
D. X's wife, in exchange for C2, gives X a certain type of affective capital (C3).
E. The capital C3 that X receives from his wife causes an increase in his level of self-approval.
F. The increase in his level of self-approval generates, in the same proportion, an increase in X's level of self-esteem.

Correlation 2:

A. The human system K pays for a consultation with a nutritionist and follows a diet.

B. K pays the annual fee of a gym membership and decides to take spinning classes every day.
C. K buy a dietary supplement online to burn fat.
D. One year later, due to the diet, the spinning classes, and the dietary supplement, K manages to achieve the desired physical appearance.
E. Because K acquires the desired physical appearance, his level of self-approval increases.
F. The increase in his level of self-approval generates, in the same proportion, an increase in K's level of self-esteem.

Now, we will express the same correlation using the concept of capital:

A. The human system K uses his monetary capital (C1) to consume external professional capital (C2) with the purpose of improving his dietary capital (C3).
B. K uses C1 to consume external professional capital (C4) with the purpose of improving his physical capital (C5).
C. K uses C1 to consume dietary capital (C3) that can help him burn fat.
D. One year later, because of the phenomena A, B, and C, K achieves the desired corporal aesthetic capital (C6).
E. Because K acquires C6, his level of self-approval increases.
F. The increase in his level of self-approval generates, in the same proportion, an increase in K's level of self-esteem.

Correlation 3:

A. The human system W works as an employee at a restaurant to pay for her college education.
B. After years of effort and sacrifice, she manages to graduate as a chemical engineer.
C. Obtaining her degree in chemical engineering increases her level of self-approval.
D. The increase in her level of self-approval generates, in the same proportion, an increase in her level of self-esteem.

Now, we will express correlation 3 using the concept of capital:

A. The human system W uses her professional capital (C1) to acquire a certain amount of monetary capital (C2) that she will spend to consume external professional, educational capital (C3).

B. After years of effort and sacrifice, W demonstrates that she has acquired the necessary intellectual and professional capital to obtain a higher level of educational capital (C4).

C. When W acquires the desired educational capital, her level of self-approval increases.

D. The increase in her level of self-approval generates, in the same proportion, an increase in her level of self-esteem.

Correlation 4:

A. The human system Z buys stocks in a company.

B. The stocks he bought triple their original value, and he decides to sell them.

C. Due to this sale, his purchasing power grows and, as a result, his level of self-approval also increases.

D. The increase in his level of self-approval generates, in the same proportion, an increase in his level of self-esteem.

Now, we will express this correlation applying the concept of capital:

A. The human system Z invests a certain amount of monetary capital (C1) in the acquisition of a certain amount of financial capital (C2).

B. C2 triples its original value (its magnitude increases), and he decides to sell it.

C. As a result of selling C2, Z's monetary capital C1 triples its value (its magnitude increases), and this growth of his monetary capital generates an increase in Z's level of self-approval.

D. The increase in his level of self-approval generates, in the same proportion, an increase in his level of self-esteem.

I could continue offering the readers countless examples of value correlations, but I believe that the concept has already been properly illustrated. It is very interesting to notice the enormous amount of effort that human systems put into achieving a healthy (or desired) level of self-esteem.

It is worth pointing out that there are **direct and indirect factors of valuation dependency**. The first ones are the factors that directly affect the human system's self-esteem. The second ones are the factors that indirectly affect the human system's self-esteem.

Let us see the case of correlation 1 in a graphic illustration:

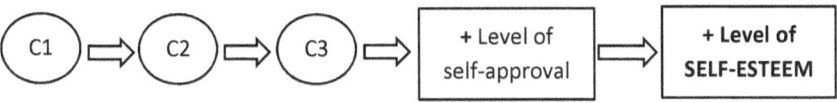

Figure 37: Examples of value correlations. Case 1.

In this example, C3 (the affective capital provided by his wife) is a direct cause of the increase or decrease of X's level of self-esteem; whereas C1 and C2 (the money and the automobile) are indirect factors of valuation dependency. In other words, the money and the automobile would not affect X's self-esteem by themselves, at all; since they are only types of capital that X interprets as functional for obtaining his wife's affection. What really interests X, to increase his self-esteem, is to obtain C3.

According to the **type of relation of dependence**, the following situations can happen in the correlations:

1) A type of capital depends on another type of capital. A factor contributes to obtaining another factor (a cause generates an effect).
2) A type of capital depends on multiple types of capital. Multiple factors contribute to obtaining another factor (multiple causes generate an effect).
3) Multiple types of capital depend on one type of capital. A factor contributes to obtaining multiple factors (a cause generates multiple effects).

To illustrate these situations, let us see the case of correlation 2 in a graphic way:

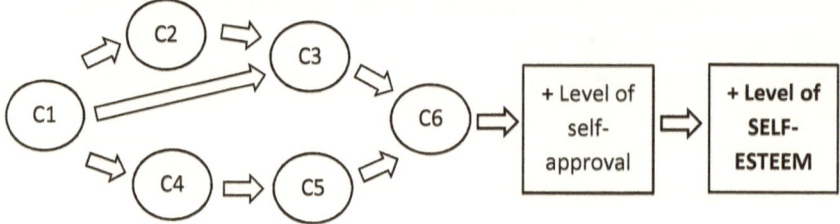

Figure 38: Examples of value correlations. Case 2.

We can see in figure 38 that the external professional capital C2 (the consultation with a nutritionist) depends on the monetary capital C1 (the money that K has to pay for the consultation). In other words, C1 is the factor that contributes to obtaining C2.

On the other hand, C6 (the desired corporal aesthetic capital) depends on multiple types of capital: the money, the consultation with the doctor, the diet, the spinning classes, the physical capital (C1, C2, C3, C4, and C5). Whereas C1 (the monetary capital) contributes to obtaining multiple types of capital in a direct manner (in the case of C2, C3, and C4) and in an indirect manner (as it happens with C5 and C6).

At the beginning of this chapter, we mentioned the variables involved in the self-esteem equation, let us illustrate them now with some examples.

Figure 39 shows the case of correlation 4:

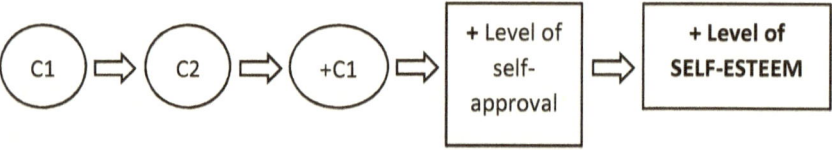

Figure 39: Examples of value correlations. Case 4.

For this human system Z, there are two types of capital involved in his self-esteem equation: the monetary capital C1 and the financial capital C2. The rise in the amount of C1 has a direct influence on the increase in his level of self-esteem. C2 depends on C1 and, in turn, the rise in the amount of C1 depends on the increase in the value of C2. The phenomenic sequence that has been mentioned requires a diversity of capital of three points to satisfy the self-esteem equation.

Correlation 4: Variables of the self-esteem equation

Amount of capital: C2 and C1 triple their value.	Types of capital: Two. Monetary capital and financial capital.	Relations of dependence: C2 depends on C1. The increase in C1 depends on the increase in C2.	Diversity of capital: Three.

Figure 40: Variables of the self-esteem equation. Case 4.

It should be noted that a person's self-esteem equation can be formed by one or several algorithms that express different value correlations.

There are simple and complex self-esteem equations. A simple equation, for example, may be constituted by only one algorithm. A complex equation, for instance, may have five different algorithms that affect the person's self-esteem.

The correlations expressed here (1, 2, 3, and 4) could all be part of a certain person's same self-esteem equation.

A human system may seek to satisfy several algorithms that constitute its self-esteem equation, manifested by different value correlations.

The complexity of the self-esteem equation increases when the number of value correlations is higher and when the values of the different variables that define them are higher.[11]

There is another aspect in the self-esteem equation that has not been mentioned, on purpose, to be addressed in the following chapter with the importance it deserves. That aspect is called value competition.

---

[11]   The number of value correlations represent another variable that defines the self-esteem equation, but we address it separately.

Value competition

All valuations are relative and, for that reason, self-valuation is relative.

This implies that the human system experiences a certain level of self-esteem based on a certain comparative evaluation that it makes in relation to one or more human systems.

In this evaluation, if its self-esteem increases, that means that its positive self-valuation is superior to one or more human systems in comparison. On the contrary, if its self-esteem decreases, that means that its positive self-valuation is inferior to one or more human systems in comparison.

Competition is the act and effect of competing.

To **compete** is to perform an action in order to obtain a relatively superior valuation in relation to one or more positively valued factors.

Every phenomenon of competition implies a **value competition**, which is determined by a comparative evaluation between the rival agents.

There are three **types of valuation judgments that human systems can generate in the value competition**, according to their particular belief systems: valuation equality, valuation superiority, or valuation inferiority.

Valuation equality is a valuation judgment that is generated when the human system carries out a comparative evaluation, according to a certain criterion, which determines that the amount and types of capital in dispute are equivalent between the rival agents.

Valuation superiority is a valuation judgment that is generated when the human system carries out a comparative evaluation, according to a certain criterion, which determines that one of the agents has a superior valuation in relation to one or more rival agents. The relative valuation superiority is generated over a difference in the amount of capital, over the lack of a certain type of capital, or over the possession of a defect or a type of anticapital. **Anticapital** is a negative factor of reality that, when possessed and accumulated, increases the level of negative self-valuation of its owner.

Valuation inferiority is a valuation judgment that is generated when the human system carries out a comparative evaluation, according to a certain criterion, which determines that one of the agents has an inferior valuation in relation to one or more rival agents. The relative valuation inferiority is generated over a difference in the amount of capital, over the lack of a certain type of capital, or over the possession of a defect or a type of anticapital.

Let us see an easy example of a person with a simple, dependent self-esteem equation, based on only one type of capital (C1), within the framework of a value competition. In this case, the protagonist human system (A) compares itself with another human system (B). In this framework of competition, the comparative evaluation may generate three possible results:

1. If A perceives a **comparative equivalence** in the possession of C1, it generates a **judgment of valuation equality** regarding B.

2. If A perceives a **comparative advantage** in the possession of C1, it generates a **judgment of valuation superiority** regarding B.

3. If A perceives a **comparative disadvantage** in the possession of C1, it generates a **judgment of valuation inferiority** regarding B.

It is worth noting that a human system can compare its situation not only with other external agents, but also with itself. A person can compare its present to its past and determine if the situation regarding one or more types of capital has improved, deteriorated, or continues being the same; and, according to its particular self-esteem equation, an increase, decrease, or preservation of the present level of positive self-valuation will take place.

Let us suppose that the monetary capital is the only factor in a person's self-esteem equation. In this case, her self-esteem will increase or decrease as she compares the amount of money (amount of monetary capital) that she has with the rest of the human systems that surround her. If she has more money than the human systems with whom she compares herself in a certain social system, she will emit judgments of valuation superiority toward her own person; for example: "I am more valuable, because I have more money than the rest." If this same person compares herself with a group of human systems in another social system and she perceives that they have more money than her, she will emit judgments of valuation inferiority; for example: "I am less valuable, because I have less money than the rest." If she compares herself and notices that everyone has a similar amount of money, she will emit judgments of valuation equality, such as: "I am just as important as the rest." Besides, her self-esteem can increase or decrease if she compares the amount of money she possesses now with the amount of money she had in the past; for example: "now, I am more important, because I have more money than last year."

In conclusion, all the weighting judgments that a human system makes obey to a comparative evaluation, guided by certain criteria of valuation that are present in its particular valuation system.

As explained before, the valuation system is an entity that justifies its existence and functions as a whole through the interaction of the subsystems of internal and external valuation.

The internal valuation subsystem (or self-valuation subsystem) is responsible for the emission of self-valuation judgments, and the external valuation subsystem is responsible for emitting weighting judgments about all kinds of external phenomena.

The understanding of this belief subsystem is of vital relevance to understand the origin of decisions and the origin of the manifestation structure generated by the definition of certain hierarchies of valuations, needs, and ends.

In this sense, the self-esteem equation is of fundamental importance for the understanding of the decisions that the human system makes.

Before concluding this chapter, we will explain the concept of anticapital a bit further. We have seen how the concept of capital helps us define factors that are positively valued. We have also mentioned the existence of factors that are negatively valued, which may be called anticapital.

Anticapital is a prejudicial factor that, when possessed and accumulated, contributes to diminishing the person's self-esteem and generating a negative self-valuation.

The definition of what constitutes capital and anticapital corresponds with the subjective criterion of the (individual or collective) protagonist human system. The distinction between the beneficial and prejudicial factors of reality are left to the discretion of the agents that interact according to their particular self-esteem equations. These agents may be individual or social persons.

Anticapital is the antinomy of capital. For example, regarding intellectual capital, its anticapital is ignorance. Regarding ethical capital, its anticapital is the lack of ethics, expressed in the level of development of the vices that a human system has. Regarding corporal aesthetic capital, the type of anticapital is the degree of corporal ugliness that a human system manifests.

In this sense, the higher the amount of anticapital that a certain human system possesses, the lower the level of self-esteem; and the lower the amount of anticapital that a certain human system possesses, the higher the level of self-esteem.

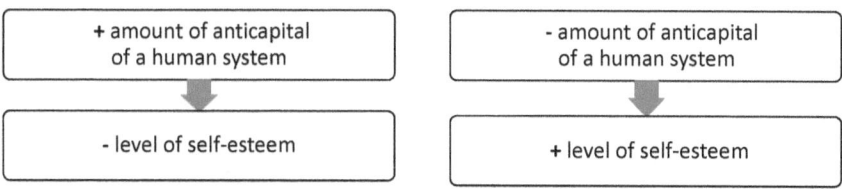

Figure 41: Correlation between anticapital and self-esteem.

The lack of certain types of capital generates a certain level of self-rejection that contributes to the dissatisfaction of the self-esteem equation.

Negative self-valuation may provoke in the human system a series of negative behaviors, which can be harmful for itself and its environment.

The viability evaluation system

The **viability evaluation system** is an entity that justifies its existence and functions as a whole through the interaction of the internal viability evaluation system and the external viability evaluation system.

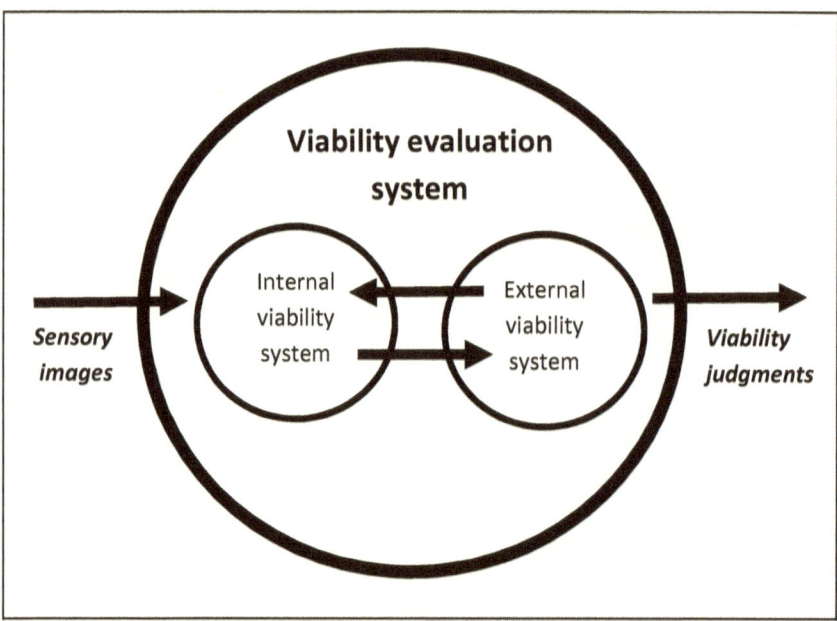

Figure 42: Viability evaluation system.

From this point forward, to simplify the terminology, the viability evaluation system will also be referred to as "viability system," and its subsystems will be called "internal viability system" and "external viability system."

The **internal viability subsystem** is constituted by criteria of viability and inviability regarding the internal reality of the protagonist human system.

The **external viability subsystem** is constituted by criteria of viability and inviability regarding the external reality of the protagonist human system.

The **criteria of viability** are associations of normative beliefs that determine the diverse viability judgments about certain phenomena of the human system's reality.

The **criteria of inviability** are associations of normative beliefs that determine the diverse inviability judgments about certain phenomena of the human system's reality.

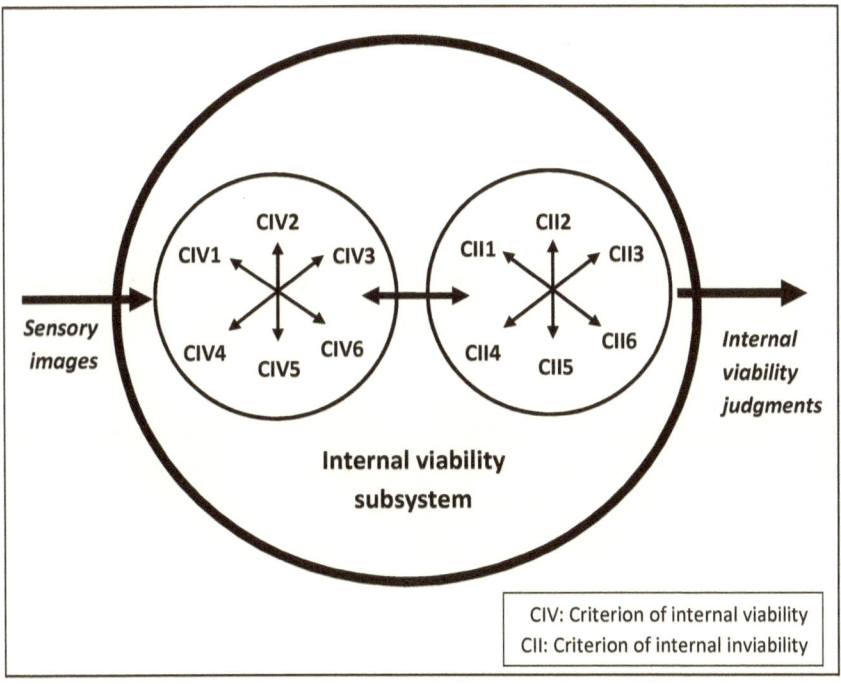

Figure 43: Internal viability subsystem.

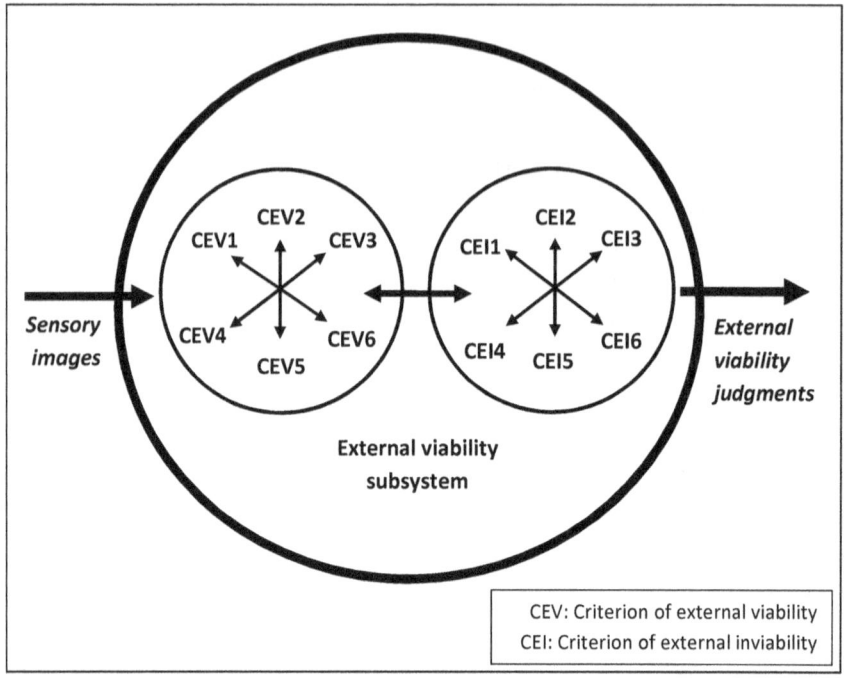

Figure 44: External viability subsystem.

According to the **law of subjective viability**, the human system determines the set of options of manifestation that it may be able to materialize according to its own belief structure.

Depending on the evaluation performed by the belief system, the human system will determine which options are more or less probable and which ones are more or less improbable, and this calculation will have a great impact on its decisions.

The **viability** is the probability that a human system will be able to materialize a certain objective, according to the endogenous and exogenous systems that enable it and restrict it. There are different degrees of viability.

The **inviability** is the improbability that a human system will be able to materialize a certain objective, according to the endogenous and exogenous systems that enable it and restrict it.

If the inviability is considered insurmountable, it is deemed as absolute; since it is impossible to achieve the contemplated option.

If the inviability is considered surmountable, it can be evaluated according to different degrees. This happens when the inviability is temporary and subject to obtaining certain resources. If the protagonist obtains the necessary resources in a certain timespan, the inviable option can become viable.

In the decision making process, only the options that the human system subjectively perceives as viable or considers to be of a superable inviability, according to its particular viability system, will be the ones that it will contemplate as options of manifestation to choose from.

It is strictly subjective and, therefore, it depends on the particular analysis made by the human system.

If the person interprets that the option is viable, it will possess a certain level of viability.

The **level of viability** is the degree of relative facileness to get the option evaluated by the human system.

The **degree of facileness** is the relative magnitude of resources that enable a human system to materialize a certain option.

If the person considers that the option is of a superable inviability, it will be able to determine its level of inviability.

The **level of inviability** is the degree of relative difficulty to get the option evaluated by the human system.

The **degree of difficulty** is the relative magnitude of constraints that restrict a human system to materialize a certain option.

We know that human systems, in their possibilities of manifestation and development, are limited by their resources and constraints.

The dichotomy between viability and inviability is useful for dividing the options in two groups (viable options and inviable options) according to the resources and constraints that define these categories, respectively.

Resources are different types of means that enable the development of certain actions.

Constraints are different types of restrictions on the human system's actions and, therefore, on its possibilities of manifestation.

The resources and constraints of a certain person are part of the endogenous and exogenous systems that define it.

Let us remember that the endogenous system defines the human system's internal reality and the exogenous system defines the external reality that affects the human system. In the group of the endogenous systems we find the mental system and the body system. In the group of the exogenous systems we find the natural, artificial, and state systems.

When the person determines its options of manifestation, its viability evaluation system contemplates the resources and constraints (internal and external) that enable and restrict the viability of the options, respectively.

The higher the magnitude of the resources that enable the human system to obtain a certain option, the higher the level of facileness, probability, and therefore, viability of that option. The lower the magnitude of the resources that enable the human system to obtain a certain option, the lower the level of facileness, probability, and therefore, viability of that option.[12]

---

[12]   These four variables are relative, since they imply a comparative evaluation.

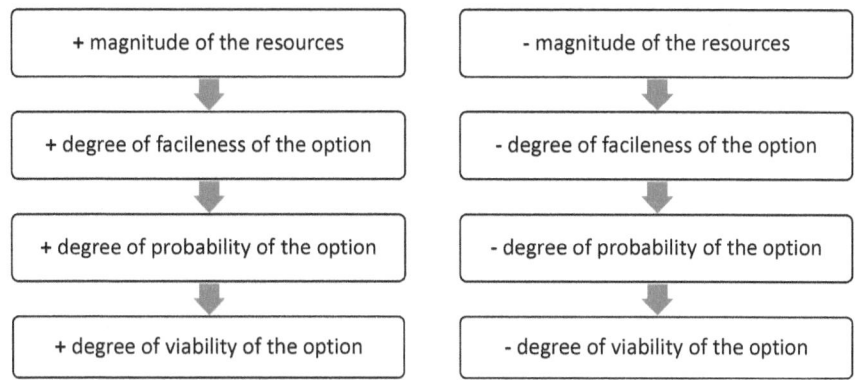

Figure 45: Correlation between resources and degree of viability.

On the other hand, the higher the magnitude of the constraints that restrict the human system to obtain a certain option, the higher the level of difficulty, improbability, and therefore, inviability of the option. The lower the magnitude of the constraints that restrict the human system to obtain that option, the lower the level of difficulty, improbability, and therefore, inviability of the option.

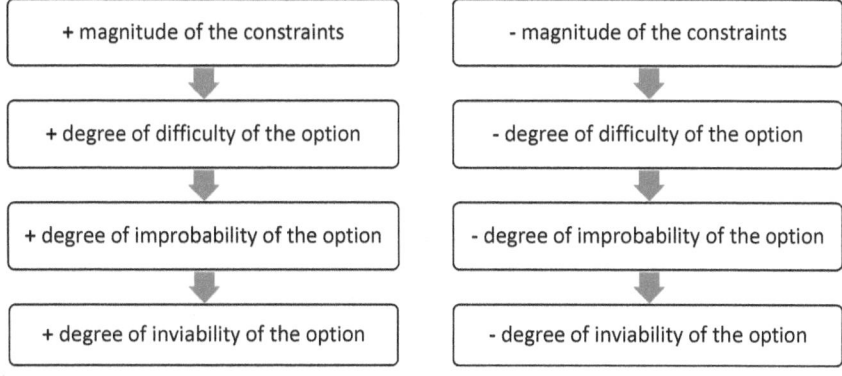

Figure 46: Correlation between constraints and degree of inviability.

The **criteria of internal viability** are associations of beliefs responsible for detecting the internal resources that enable the human system to manifest the option it is contemplating.

The **criteria of external viability** are associations of beliefs responsible for detecting the external resources that enable the human system to manifest the option it is contemplating.

The **criteria of internal inviability** are associations of beliefs responsible for identifying the internal constraints that limit the human system's manifestation of the option it is contemplating.

The **criteria of external inviability** are associations of beliefs responsible for identifying the external constraints that restrict the human system in the attainment of the option it is contemplating.

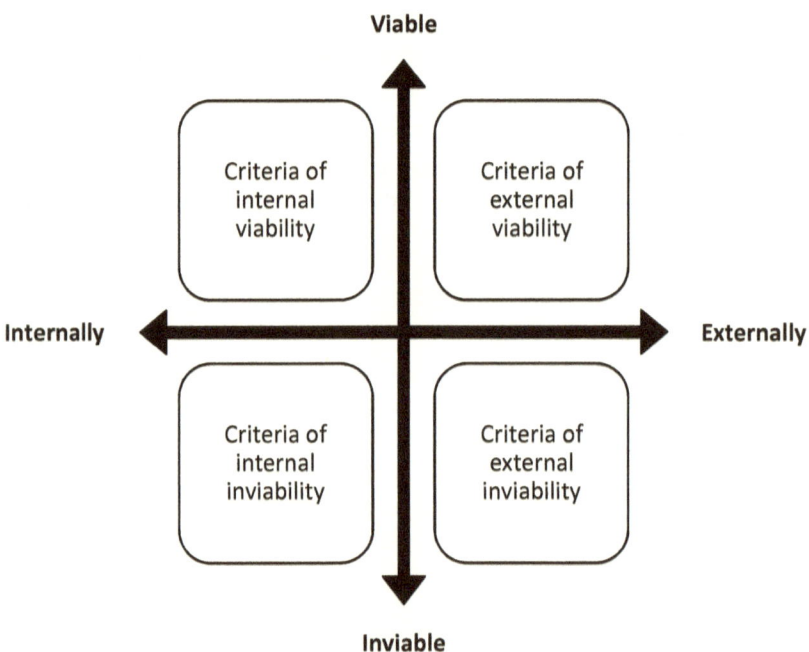

Figure 47: Map of criteria of viability and inviability.

A possible analysis to determine the level of viability of the options can be performed by answering these four questions:

1. What resources (internal and external) are necessary for the option X to be viable?

2. Of the resources mentioned above, which ones do I have and which ones do I not have?
3. Of the resources that I do not have, which ones can I get?
4. How long would it take to get those resources?

These four questions should be repeated for each option of manifestation that is being contemplated.

In order to answer question 1, it will be useful to list the internal and external resources that are needed to obtain that option.

From the resources listed in question 1, the human system will evaluate which one of them it possesses. The ones that it does not have will become constraints.

Once the current resources and constraints are contemplated, the person will evaluate which of the constraints are superable, what is required to surmount them and how long it takes to do it.

The map of resources and constraints (internal and external) is a very useful tool to perform this evaluation, since it contributes to analyzing the viability conditions of each one of the contemplated options. As we can see in figure 48, the graphic is derived from the map of criteria of viability and inviability (figure 47).

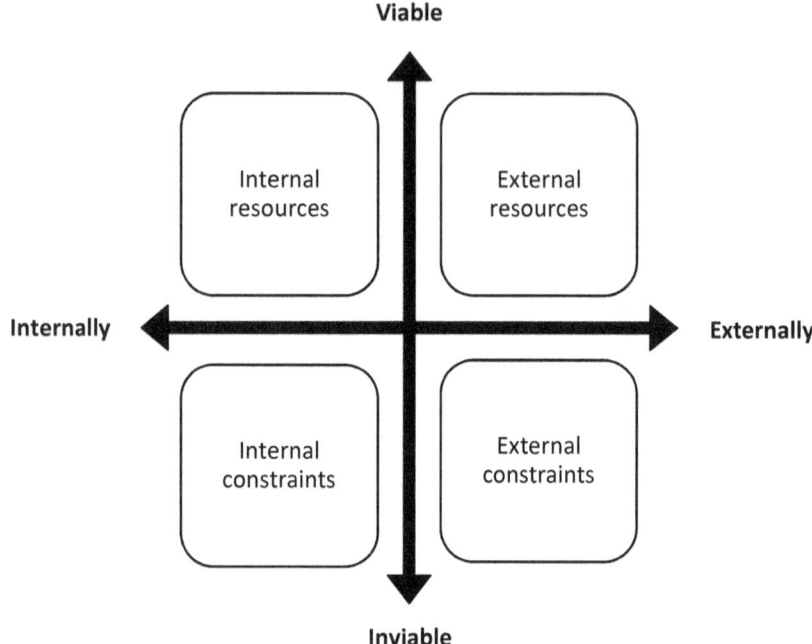

Figure 48: Map of resources and constraints.

The map of resources and constraints can be used to more accurately evaluate a person's capacity to achieve a certain option of manifestation in due time and manner, or to understand and expand the range of viable options that the protagonist human system can enjoy.

This tool highlights the value of understanding the internal and external circumstances that enable or incapacitate an individual, or a social system, to generate certain type of decisions and behaviors and to experience certain situations.

There are results that can be achieved and there are results that are unattainable. Acknowledging this difference is fundamental to avoid wasting energy on an impossible objective and, additionally, to design a plan that aims at getting the means that are lacking and/or overcoming the constraints that limit the achievement of the desired end.

According to the **law of conditioned options**, the number of viable options of manifestation of a particular protagonist human system depends on the diversity and the level of development of the resources it has.

In this sense, the higher the diversity and level of development of the resources that a human system possesses, the higher the number of viable options of manifestation that will be available for it. The lower the diversity and level of development of the resources that a human system possesses, the lower the number of viable options of manifestation that will be available for it.

On the other hand, the higher the diversity and level of development of the constraints, the lower the number of viable options of manifestation that will be available. The lower the diversity and level of development of the constraints, the higher the number of viable options of manifestation that the protagonist human system will have.

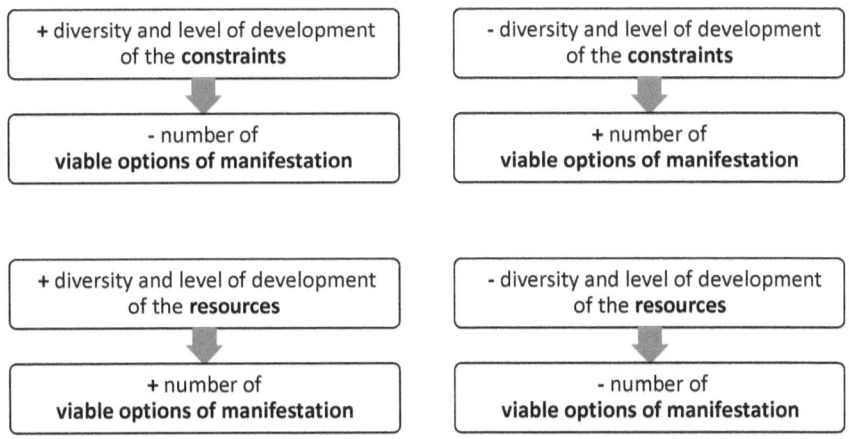

Figure 49: Law of conditioned options.

In the next chapter, we will offer different typologies that will help us understand the variables for the viability analysis of the options.

Typologies for the viability analysis

Types of constraints and resources

There are different types of constraints and resources that affect the human systems' possibilities of manifestation. In the next pages, we will mention some of them.

This categorization is useful for studying different cases that require analyzing diverse maps of resources and constraints.

Superable constraints are all the restrictions that the human system is able to overcome by acquiring certain resources.

Insuperable constraints are all the restrictions that the human system is not able to overcome.

Mutable constraints are all the restrictions that are susceptible to be modified by certain actions.

Immutable constraints are all the restrictions that are not susceptible to be modified by certain actions.

Internal constraints are all the restrictions that the human system has in its internal reality. Internal constraints are divided into corporal and mental constraints.

Corporal constraints are all the restrictions that the human system has in its body system.

Mental constraints are all the restrictions that the human system has in its mental system.

External constraints are all the restrictions that the human system has in its external reality.

Natural constraints are all the restrictions that the human system has in relation to natural systems.

Artificial constraints are all the restrictions that the human system has in relation to artificial systems.

State constraints are all the restrictions that the human system has in relation to state systems.

Human constraints are all the restrictions that the human system experiences due to certain human systems that affect it. Human constraints are divided into individual and social constraints.

Individual constraints are all the restrictions that the human system experiences due to certain individual human systems that affect it.

Social constraints are all the restrictions that the human system experiences due to certain social systems that affect it.

Economic constraints are all the restrictions that the human system experiences in relation to the economic system.

Juridical constraints are all the restrictions that the human system experiences in relation to the juridical system.

Political constraints are all the restrictions that the human system experiences in relation to the political system.

Family constraints are all the restrictions that the human system experiences in relation to the family system.

Religious constraints are all the restrictions that the human system experiences in relation to the religious system.

Marital constraints are all the restrictions that the human system experiences in relation to the marital system.

Educational constraints are all the restrictions that the human system experiences in relation to the educational system.

Military constraints are all the restrictions that the human system experiences in relation to the military system.

Security constraints are all the restrictions that the human system experiences in relation to the security system.

Sanitary constraints are all the restrictions that the human system experiences in relation to the sanitary system.

Business constraints are all the restrictions that the human system experiences in relation to the business system.

Work constraints are all the restrictions that the human system experiences in relation to the work system.

Tax constraints are all the restrictions that the human system experiences in relation to the tax system.

Let us now look at the list of types of resources.

Internal resources are all the means that the human system has in its internal reality. The internal reality is composed of the will (or soul), the mental system, and the body system.

Mental resources are all the means that the human system has in its mental system.

Corporal resources are all the means that the human system has in its body system.

External resources are all the means that are part of the human system's external reality.

State resources are all the means that the human system has in relation to the state system.

Natural resources are all the means that the human system has in relation to the natural system.

Artificial resources are all the means that the human system has in relation to the artificial system.

Human resources are all the human means that a person uses to achieve an objective. Human resources are divided into individual and social resources.

Individual human resources are all the individuals (individual means) that a human system uses to achieve an objective.

Social human resources are all the social means that a human system uses to achieve an objective.

Economic resources are all the economic means that a human system uses to achieve an objective.

Business resources are all the means available to a company that a human system uses to achieve an objective.

Professional resources are all the professional means that a human system uses to achieve an objective.

Family resources are all the family means that a human system uses to achieve an objective.

Marital resources are all the marital means that a human system uses to achieve an objective.

Political resources are all the political means that a human system uses to achieve an objective.

Juridical resources are all the juridical means that a human system uses to achieve an objective.

Religious resources are all the religious means that a human system uses to achieve an objective.

Sanitary resources are all the sanitary means that a human system uses to achieve an objective.

Military resources are all the military means that a human system uses to achieve an objective.

Educational resources are all the educational means that a human system uses to achieve an objective.

The typology of constraints and resources can be extended, and it helps to cover all the cases in which different maps of resources and constraints have to be analyzed.

According to these types of constraints and resources, the human system can define its options of manifestation and place them on the map.

Types of options

The options to be studied in the viability analysis can be classified according to the categories listed below.

A **viable option** is a possibility of manifestation that has a certain level of relative probability of being achieved by the human system.

An **option of high viability** is a possibility of manifestation that has a relatively high probability of being achieved by the human system.

An **option of moderate viability** is a possibility of manifestation that has a relatively moderate probability of being achieved by the human system.

An **option of low viability** is a possibility of manifestation that has a relatively low probability of being achieved by the human system.

An **inviable option** is a possibility of manifestation that has a certain level of improbability, relative or absolute, of being achieved by the human system. Relative improbability refers to superable inviability, and absolute improbability refers to insuperable inviability.

An **option of insuperable inviability** is a possibility of manifestation that has an absolute improbability of being achieved by the human system. In this case, constraints are insuperable.

An **option of superable inviability** is a possibility of manifestation that has a certain relative improbability of being achieved by the human system. Constraints can be overcome. In this case, different levels of inviability can be mentioned.

An **option of high inviability** is a possibility of manifestation that has a relatively high improbability of being achieved by the human system.

An **option of moderate inviability** is a possibility of manifestation that has a relatively moderate improbability of being achieved by the human system.

An **option of low inviability** is a possibility of manifestation that has a relatively low improbability of being achieved by the human system.

An **internally viable option** is a possibility of manifestation that has a certain probability of being achieved by the human system, in relation to the resources of its internal reality.

An **internally inviable option** is a possibility of manifestation that has a certain improbability of being achieved by the human system, in relation to the constraints of its internal reality.

An **externally viable option** is a possibility of manifestation that has a certain probability of being achieved by the human system, in relation to the resources of its external reality.

An **externally inviable option** is a possibility of manifestation that has a certain improbability of being achieved by the human system, in relation to the constraints of its external reality.

A **rational option** is a possibility of manifestation that the human system analyzes based on certain information that has a particular degree of relative fidelity.[13]

An **option of high rationality** is a possibility of manifestation that the human system analyzes based on certain information that has a relatively high degree of fidelity.

An **option of moderate rationality** is a possibility of manifestation that the human system analyzes based on certain information that has a relatively moderate degree of fidelity.

An **option of low rationality** is a possibility of manifestation that the human system analyzes based on certain information that has a relatively low degree of fidelity.

An **irrational option** is a possibility of manifestation that the human system analyzes based on certain information that has a relative degree of inaccuracy.

An **option of high irrationality** is a possibility of manifestation that the human system analyzes based on certain information that has a relatively high degree of inaccuracy.

---

[13]   In the next chapter, we will develop the subjects of rationality and fidelity of the information.

An **option of moderate irrationality** is a possibility of manifestation that the human system analyzes based on certain information that has a relatively moderate degree of inaccuracy.

An **option of low irrationality** is a possibility of manifestation that the human system analyzes based on certain information that has a relatively low degree of inaccuracy.

A **conscious option** is a possibility of manifestation that the human system analyzes and acknowledges in the decision process.

An **unconscious option** is a possibility of manifestation that the human system analyzes but does not acknowledge in the decision process.

A **contemplated option** is a possibility of manifestation that the human system analyzes in the decision process.

A **non-contemplated option** is a possibility of manifestation that the human system does not analyze in the decision process.

A **selected option** is a possibility of manifestation that the human system chooses to develop in the decision process.

A **non-selected option** is a possibility of manifestation that the human system does not choose to develop in the decision process.

Types of viability and inviability according to time parameters

The types of viability and inviability always serve to categorize the contemplated options according to their characteristics and their connection with the resources and constraints of the human system that wants to materialize them.

The viability of an option may vary in the future, and that affects the decision making. Since the viability analysis is performed at a specific moment in time, the variable of time plays a key role.

In this case, I will name the types of viability and inviability according to their specific time limit. Let us look at the brief list below.

Temporarily limited viability: The option has a relatively limited execution time, due to the constraints experienced by the human system.

Short-term viability: The option has a short-term execution time, due to the constraints experienced by the human system. When that timespan is over, the option is no longer viable.

Medium-term viability: The option has a medium-term execution time, due to the constraints experienced by the human system. When that timespan is over, the option is no longer viable.

Long-term viability: The option has a long-term execution time, due to the constraints experienced by the human system. When that timespan is over, the option is no longer viable.

Immediate viability: The option can be executed immediately.

Delayed viability: The option cannot be executed immediately; on the contrary, it takes a certain period of time to be able to perform it.

Immediate inviability: The option cannot be executed immediately.

Delayed inviability: The possibility of executing the option expires after a certain period of time.

Temporarily limited inviability: The option cannot be executed until a certain period of time passes. When that timespan is over, the option becomes viable for the protagonist human system.

Short-term inviability: For a short period of time, the option cannot be executed. When that timespan is over, the option becomes viable for the human system.

Medium-term inviability: The option cannot be executed for a medium period of time. When that timespan is over, the option becomes viable for the human system.

Long-term inviability: The option cannot be executed for a long period of time. When that timespan is over, the option becomes viable for the human system.

Information and decision criteria

A **judgment** is an evaluation of a certain phenomenon made by the human system on the basis of certain type of information.

An **evaluation** is the assignment of characteristics to the judged phenomenon according to the criteria employed by the evaluating human system.

Criteria are associations of normative beliefs that enable the assignment of diverse linguistic meanings to a certain set of sensory images that are logically connected with them. Criteria are a set of rules that determine the different types of evaluations according to the different sensory stimuli that the human system perceives.

Decision criteria are composed of the criteria of valuation and the criteria of viability evaluation.

The **criteria of valuation** are associations of normative valuation beliefs that constitute the valuation subsystems and contribute to generating several valuation judgments about the different elements of reality that define the human system and its environment.

The criteria of valuation are a set of arguments that contribute to the validation, or not, to some degree, of all the factors of reality. The factors that are validated have a positive valuation, and the factors that are invalidated have a negative valuation. The factors of the environment are judged by the criteria of external valuation, and the factors of the internal reality are judged by the criteria of internal valuation.

The **criteria of viability evaluation** include the criteria of viability and the criteria of inviability.

The criteria of viability are associations of normative beliefs that determine the diverse viability judgments about certain phenomena of the human system's internal and external reality. The criteria of inviability are associations of normative beliefs that determine the diverse inviability judgments about certain phenomena of the human system's internal and external reality.

Decision criteria				
	Criteria of valuation		Criteria of viability evaluation	
Internal	Criteria of positive valuation	Criteria of negative valuation	Criteria of viability	Criteria of inviability
External				

Figure 50: Decision criteria.

The decision criteria are constituted on the basis of certain type of information, expressed in the form of sensory stimuli, which conditions and shapes the protagonist human system's belief structure.

The information that shapes the criteria enters the mental system through a set of stimuli, which depend on the education that the human system has experienced through the process of formal and informal socialization, in addition to its own self-taught capacity.

The **socialization process** is a phenomenon by which the members of a social system are educated to make their respective belief structures compatible with the belief structure of the community. Through this mechanism, the social system conditions its members and requires them to adopt certain options of thoughts and behaviors that are consistent with the structure of collective beliefs. The socialization process is divided into formal and informal socialization.

Formal socialization is the socialization process that derives from the formal educational system.

The formal educational system is constituted by the pre-school educational system, the primary educational system, the secondary educational system, and the university educational system. The political system is the one responsible for the formal socialization process, because the educational policies and laws come from the political system.

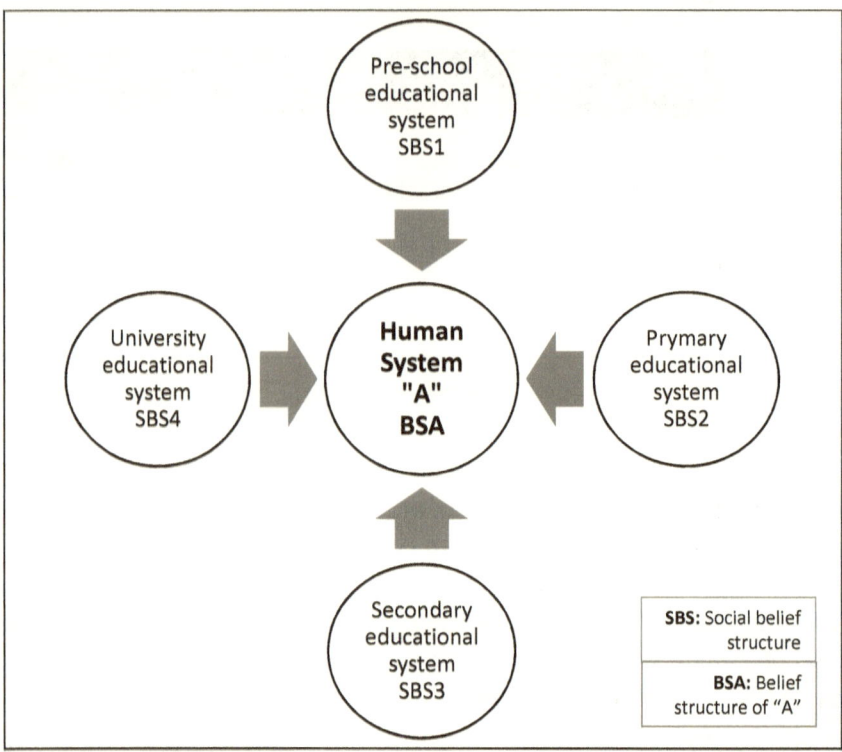

Figure 51: Formal socialization process.

Informal socialization is the socialization process that derives from the informal educational system.

The informal educational system is constituted by families, sports clubs, groups of friends, mass media, and political parties, among others. As we can see, different types of social systems are responsible for the informal socialization process.

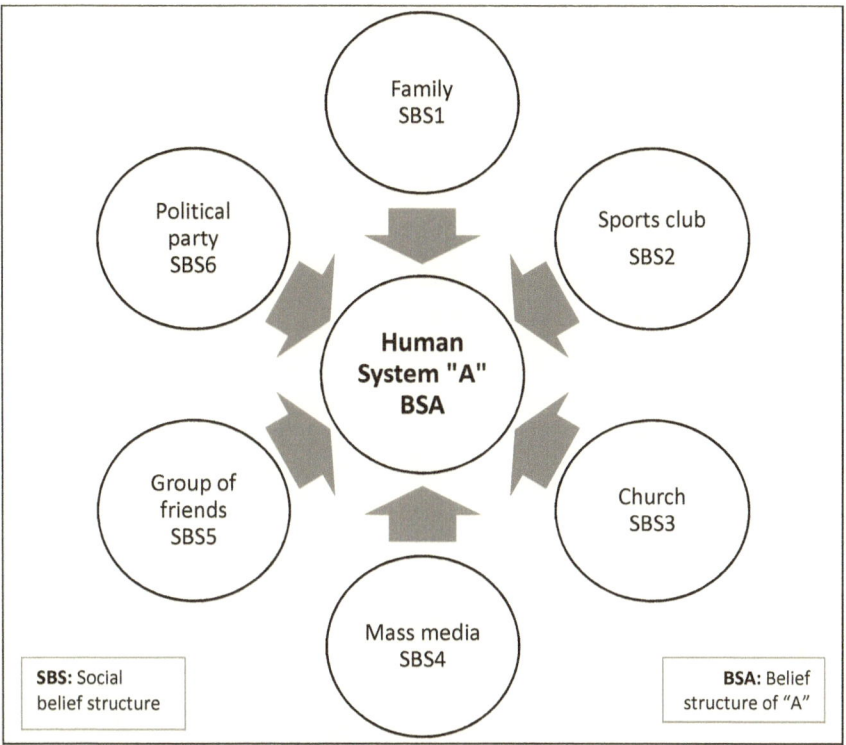

Figure 52: Informal socialization process.

We have pointed out that the criteria on which the human system emits a decision are built on the basis of certain type of information.

Information is defined as a set of data about different phenomena that can have several levels of fidelity.[14]

The **data** are the sensory images that proceed from the human system's internal or external reality, decoded according to its particular active belief system. A belief subsystem that is fundamental in the decoding of all data is the linguistic communication system.

---

[14]   The socialization process and the subject of the fidelity of the information will be also explained in the book *Social Systems Theory. A model based on Mental Systems* (see the section "Related works" at the end of this book).

Fidelity is the degree of relative accuracy that certain information possesses.

Accuracy refers to the degree of assertive rigorousness of the analyzed data.

The assertive rigorousness depends on four variables:

- The degree of justification
- The degree of corroboration
- The degree of internal coherence
- The degree of external coherence

The **justification** is the argumentative explanation, logically developed, that supports a criterion.

The higher the degree of justification, the higher the degree of assertive rigorousness of the analyzed data. The lower the degree of justification, the lower the degree of assertive rigorousness of the analyzed data.

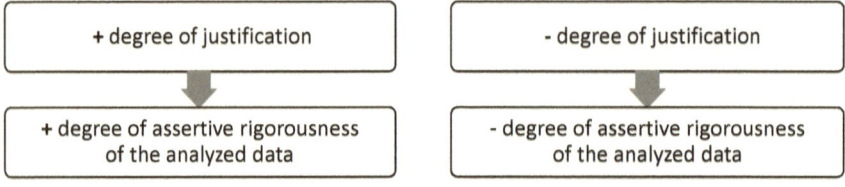

Figure 53: Correlation between justification and assertive rigorousness.

The **corroboration** is the empirical evidence that supports the justification.

The higher the degree of corroboration, the higher the degree of assertive rigorousness of the analyzed data. The lower the degree of corroboration, the lower the degree of assertive rigorousness of the analyzed data.

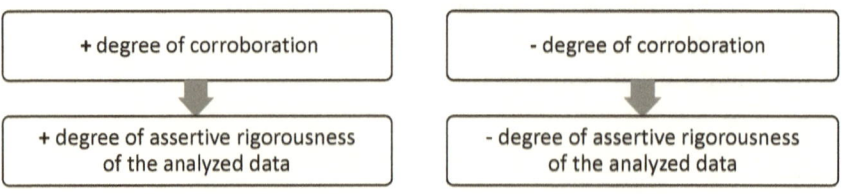

Figure 54: Correlation between corroboration and assertive rigorousness.

The **internal coherence** is the degree of associative logic of the ideas that constitute the analyzed data. The higher the degree of associative logic of the analyzed data, the higher their degree of internal coherence. The lower the degree of associative logic of the analyzed data, the lower their degree of internal coherence.

In turn, the higher the degree of internal coherence, the higher the degree of assertive rigorousness of the analyzed data. The lower the degree of internal coherence, the lower the degree of assertive rigorousness of the analyzed data.

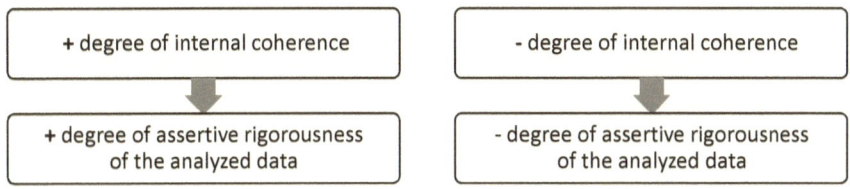

Figure 55: Correlation between internal coherence and assertive rigorousness.

The **external coherence** is the degree of associative logic that exists between the analyzed data and the phenomena of reality that they represent. The higher the degree of correspondence between the analyzed data and the phenomena of reality that they represent, the higher the degree of external coherence. The lower the degree of correspondence between the analyzed data and the phenomena of reality that they represent, the lower the degree of external coherence.

In turn, the higher the degree of external coherence, the higher the degree of assertive rigorousness of the analyzed data. The lower the degree of external coherence, the lower the degree of assertive rigorousness of the analyzed data.

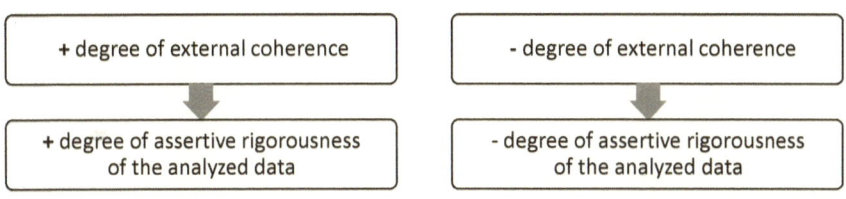

Figure 56: Correlation between external coherence and assertive rigorousness.

In order to simplify the study of the level of relative fidelity of the information, we will use the variables of justification and corroboration, according to absolute values represented by four possible options:

A) Presence of justification
B) Presence of corroboration
C) Absence of justification
D) Absence of corroboration

The fidelity of the information is relatively high when it has justification and corroboration.

The fidelity of the information is relatively moderate when it has justification but it lacks corroboration.

The fidelity of the information is relatively low when it lacks justification and corroboration.

Level of fidelity of the information		
LEVEL OF FIDELITY	*Justification*	*Corroboration*
High	Justified information	Corroborated information
Moderate	Justified information	Uncorroborated information
Low	Information not justified	Uncorroborated information

Figure 57: Level of fidelity of the information.

The type of information will contribute to the development of certain criteria, and, in turn, the criteria will decode the information that the person receives. However, at the beginning, the criteria are formed according to the information obtained.

The fidelity of the information will determine the degree of fidelity of the criterion, and the degree of fidelity of the criterion will determine the degree of fidelity of the decision process.

The higher the level of fidelity of the information, the higher the degree of fidelity of the criterion which is developed on its basis, and, therefore, the higher the level of fidelity of the decision process. The lower the level of fidelity of the information, the lower the degree of fidelity of the criterion that is developed on its basis, and, therefore, the lower the level of fidelity of the decision process.

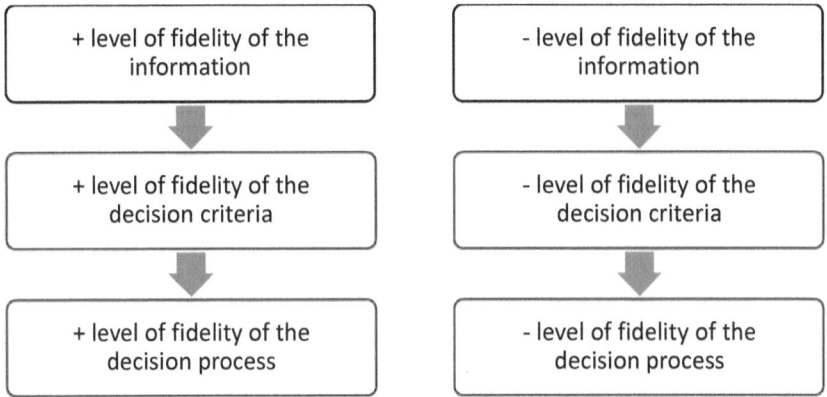

Figure 58: Correlation between fidelity of the information, the criteria, and the decision process.

The concept of fidelity of the decision process serves to analyze the level of risk related to this phenomenon.

Risk is the probability that an expectation, expressed through an end, is not fulfilled.

For a protagonist human system, taking a risk is venturing to experience a situation in which the expectation may not be fulfilled.

Risk implies uncertainty, and it is always present. In order to minimize it, a person can improve the evaluation process, perfect the analysis mechanisms, and increase the levels of fidelity of the information through which the decision criteria are formed.

The higher the level of fidelity of the decision process, the lower the level of risk regarding the desired result; that is to say, the lower the probability of not fulfilling the expectations expressed in the projective thought that defines the decision.

On the contrary, the lower the level of fidelity of the decision process, the higher the level of risk regarding the desired result; that is to say, the higher the probability of not fulfilling the expectations expressed in the projective thought that defines the decision.

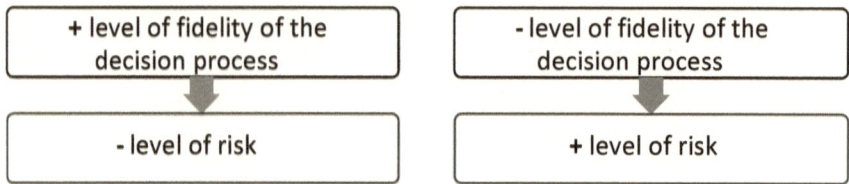

Figure 59: Correlation between the fidelity of the decision process and the level of risk.

Lastly, it is worth mentioning that there is a correspondence between the level of fidelity of the decision process and its level of rationality.

The higher the degree of fidelity of the decision process, the higher its degree of rationality. The lower the degree of fidelity of the decision process, the lower its degree of rationality.

The fidelity is the degree of relative accuracy that the information has, due to the degree of assertive rigorousness of the data.

We know that assertive rigorousness depends on four variables: justification, corroboration, internal coherence, and external coherence. The higher the levels of these variables, the higher the degree of assertive rigorousness, fidelity, and rationality of the decision process.

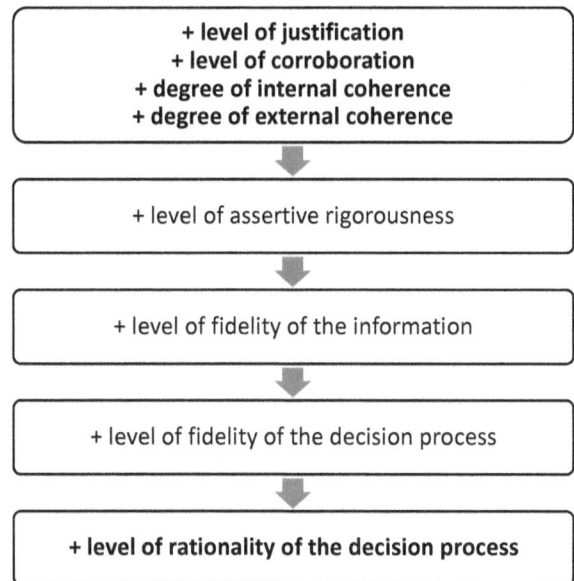

Figure 60: Correlation between the level of assertive rigorousness of the information and the degree of rationality of the decision process.

In addition, there is a parallelism between the absence of fidelity of the decision process and its irrationality.

The absence of fidelity is measured by the degree of relative inaccuracy that certain information has. The inaccuracy refers to the degree of absence of assertive rigorousness of the analyzed data.

There are four antinomies that constitute the variables of the absence of fidelity:

- Absence of justification
- Absence of corroboration
- Internal incoherence
- External incoherence

If these antinomies occur, we should not talk about degrees of rationality; instead, we should talk about degrees of irrationality in the decision process.

The higher the degree of these variables, the higher the level of absence of assertive rigorousness, lack of fidelity, and irrationality of the decision process.

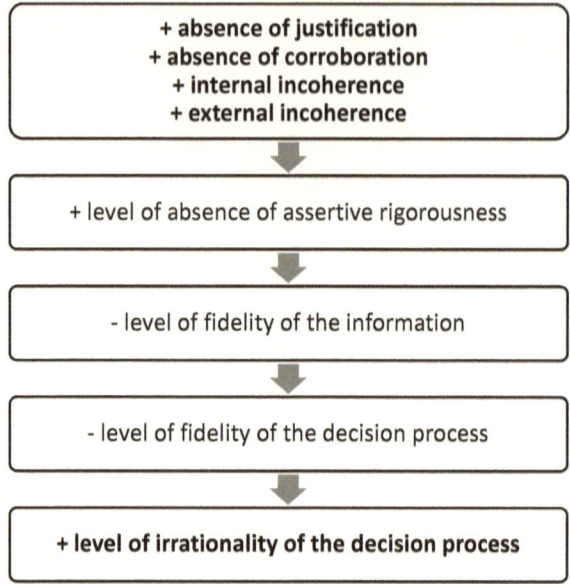

Figure 61: Correlation between the lack of assertive rigorousness of the information and the degree of irrationality of the decision process.

In summary, we can define **rationality** as the degree of fidelity of the decision criteria that the human system employs for the development of several teleological behaviors.

Irrationality, on the contrary, is the degree of inaccuracy of the decision criteria that the human system employs for the development of several teleological behaviors.

According to this, a **rational behavior** is a physical and/or linguistic action developed on the basis of certain decision criteria that have a certain degree of fidelity.

An **irrational behavior** is a physical and/or linguistic action developed on the basis of certain decision criteria that have a certain degree of inaccuracy.

Equation of real well-being

The decision making process can be analyzed in four stages, formed by three evaluative moments that lead to the gestation of the final decision:

1. The valuation of the contemplated options.
2. The viability evaluation of the contemplated options.
3. The evaluation of the real well-being of the contemplated options.
4. The adoption of the decision.

The first stage is carried out by the valuation system, which is in charge of assigning a valuation level (positive or negative) to the contemplated options.

The second stage is performed by the viability evaluation system, which determines the level of viability or inviability of the contemplated options.

In the third stage, both systems intervene. This is where the equation of real well-being becomes relevant.

It is important to clarify that the first and the second evaluations do not necessarily happen in that order, however, the results that both provide will be determinant for the analysis of the level of real well-being of the contemplated options. Based on this last evaluation, the human system determines the thought about the future that will constitute the decision.

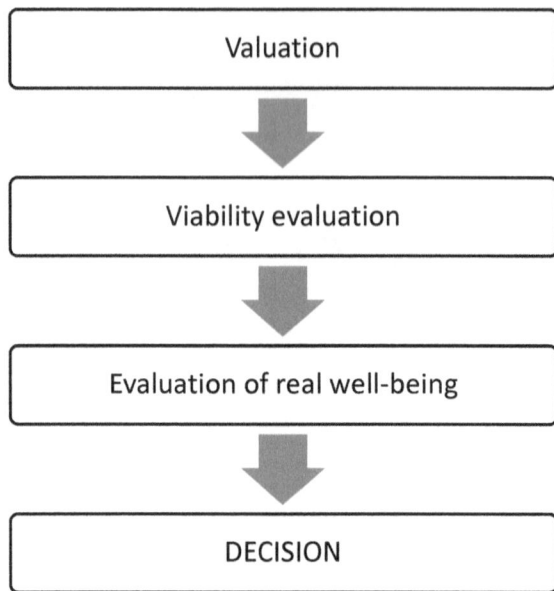

Figure 62: Stages of the decision process.

We know that the most valued thoughts about the future are the ones that the human system will choose to materialize. Furthermore, the most valued thoughts are the ones that offer the human system the highest relative level of well-being, or the lowest relative level of ill-being, according to the contemplated options about the future.

It is worth noting that the concepts of well-being and ill-being refer to different **emotional states** that human systems experience.

In addition, the viability analysis, which the person performs when evaluating the options of manifestation, will determine the degree of viability or inviability of the contemplated options.

From the combination of these variables (well-being/ill-being and viability/inviability) the **equation of real well-being** is formed. This equation will determine the option of manifestation that the human system will choose to materialize.

The relative level of real well-being offered by the contemplated options will be the key element in the conclusion of the decision process.

According to the **law of decision**, the human system will always choose the subjectively viable option that offers the highest relative level of real well-being, or the lowest relative level of real ill-being, at every moment and in certain circumstances.

The options projected by the human system offer a certain state of well-being or ill-being.

From each projected option, the person determines the potential, relative well-being that can be obtained by its acquisition. But the potential, relative well-being of the projected option is affected by its degree of projected, relative viability.

From this joint evaluation comes the concept of projected **real well-being**, which is expressed in the following equation: the level of potential well-being of the projected option minus the viability cost equals the level of real well-being of the option. It should be noted that the result of this subtraction is the projection of the level of real well-being that the option offers to the protagonist human system.

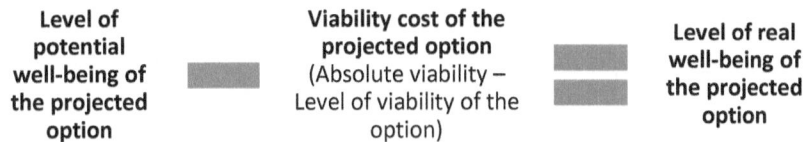

| Level of potential well-being of the projected option | | Viability cost of the projected option (Absolute viability – Level of viability of the option) | | Level of real well-being of the projected option |

Figure 63: Equation of real well-being.

The first variable, the **level of potential well-being of the projected option**, refers to the level of well-being –or ill-being, if it is a negative value– that the person feels when the experience of the contemplated option is imagined.

The second variable, the **viability cost**, refers to the relative magnitude of resources that are necessary to obtain the option evaluated by the human system. It is the result of the following subtraction: the level of absolute viability minus the level of perceived viability of the option.

The level of **absolute viability** will always be a fixed value of ten points.

The level of perceived viability of the option is the degree of facileness –or difficulty, if the value is negative– to obtain the option evaluated by the human system (according to its subjective viability analysis). If the option is considered viable, its level of facileness is analyzed, and it will receive a positive value on a scale from zero to ten. If the option is considered inviable, its level of difficulty is analyzed, and it will receive a negative value on a scale from zero to ten.[15]

The result, the **level of real well-being of the option**, is the level of projected well-being minus the viability cost.

In order to make a decision, the human system evaluates each option according to this equation and then compares the results. The option that offers the highest level of real well-being, or the lowest level of real ill-being, depending on the situation, will be the option chosen by the person.

In this sense, we can find three variations of the equation, according to the intervening variables and the results they generate.

If the contemplated option offers a certain level of projected well-being, the first variable will always be named as the "potential well-being of the projected option." In this case, the result of the equation, depending on the viability cost, can be positive or negative.

If the contemplated option offers a certain level of projected ill-being, the first variable will always be named as the "potential ill-being of the projected option." In these cases, the result of the equation is always negative.

In sum, the three variations of the equation of real well-being are:

1) The projected well-being minus the viability cost equals a certain degree of real well-being.

---

[15]   As established by the typologies of constraints and inviability, there are temporarily inviable options, but once that time span is over, the inviability can turn into viability. When the person considers that an option is inviable for a certain period of time, this means that is has superable constraints. The degree of difficulty is the cost of overcoming those constraints for the human system.

2) The projected well-being minus the viability cost equals a certain degree of real ill-being.

3) The projected ill-being minus the viability cost equals a certain degree of real ill-being.

These variations may be expressed in the following way:

1) $+ PW - VC = + RW$
2) $+ PW - VC = - RI$
3) $- PI - VC = - RI$

The level of well-being (**PW** or **RW**) is a number that in the mathematic language is represented with the positive sign.

The viability cost (**VC**) is represented with the negative sign.

The level of ill-being (**PI** or **RI**) is a number that in the mathematic language is represented with the negative sign.

In the type of equation 1, the variable of potential well-being (of a positive sign) has a higher magnitude than the variable of viability cost (of a negative sign), therefore, a positive result of real well-being is generated.

In the type of equation 2, the variable of potential well-being (of a positive sign) has a lower magnitude than the variable of viability cost (of a negative sign), therefore, a negative result of real ill-being is generated.

In the type of equation 3, the first variable is a level of potential ill-being (of a negative sign) and the second one is the viability cost (which is always equal to or less than zero); therefore, inevitably, the result will be negative, representing a level of real ill-being.

This can be synthesized in the following terms:

1) If $PW > VC \rightarrow RW$
2) If $PW \leq VC \rightarrow RI$
3) If $PI \rightarrow RI$

The equation of real well-being represents the way we evaluate the options, consciously or unconsciously, when we make a decision. The hypothetical values are useful to illustrate different cases.

It is interesting to see how the projected relative well-being or ill-being that an option can offer is negatively affected by the viability cost it implies. Human beings always contemplate the resources they must invest in order to achieve an objective. The objective can be very valuable for a person, but the investment of resources can be so costly that it generates a decrease in the level of perceived real well-being.

It is worth noting that, according to what can be deduced from the law of valuation, the level of well-being or ill-being assigned to a certain option will determine the same level of positive or negative valuation, respectively. As a consequence, the equation of projected real well-being enables the existence of the equation of projected real valuation.

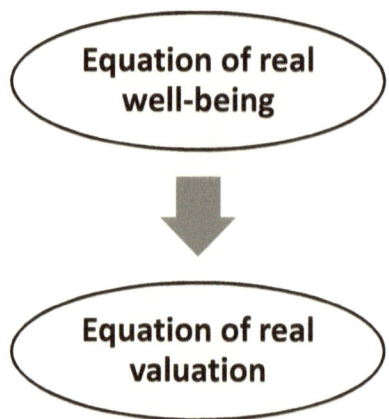

Figure 64: Equivalence between the equations
of real well-being and real valuation.

Given its equivalence with the equation of real well-being, the **equation of projected real valuation** can be expressed in the following way:

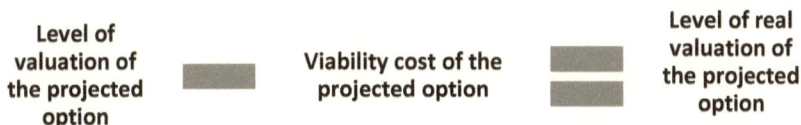

Figure 65: Equation of real valuation.

The equation of real valuation is useful to understand the definitive valuation assigned to a certain option.

Let us remember that the relative character of the valuation of an option is due to the comparative weighting that the human system makes every time it performs a valuation assessment, as explained before in the law of relative valuation.

Given a certain group of contemplated options, according to the equation of real valuation, the option that offers the relatively highest level of positive real valuation is the one that will be preferred.

However, the equation of real valuation does not always offer positive results. It can also offer negative valuations when the viability cost is higher than the level of positive valuation, or when the first variable has a level of negative valuation.

In this sense, the three variations of the equation of real valuation can be expressed in the following way (where the variable **PV** represents the level of projected valuation and the result **RV** represents the level of real valuation):

1) $+PV - VC = +RV$
2) $+PV - VC = -RV$
3) $-PV - VC = -RV$

In the case in which a set of options perceived as viable are compared and all of them offer negative results in their respective real valuations, the human system will prefer the option that minimizes the level of ill-being. In other words, the person will choose the option that has the relatively lowest level of real negative valuation.

Let us illustrate this equation and the law of decision with some very simple examples:

Case 1:

A person has the X amount of money available in the bank and she evaluates three possible, mutually exclusive actions that she can carry out with it: "I could buy a new laptop" (Y1), "I could buy a video game console" (Y2), or "I could leave the money in the bank" (Y3). When the person is mentally evaluating those thoughts about the future, her valuation system emits valuation thoughts, with the amount of relative, positive weighting of nine (V1), seven (V2), and two points (V3), respectively; derived from the identical levels of relative well-being generated by the images of herself experiencing those situations.

Projected options		Level of valuation/ well-being
1	Having a new laptop	(+) 9
2	Having a video game console	(+) 7
3	Having the money in the bank	(+) 2

Figure 66: Valuation structure. Case 1.

For the first two options, the perceived viability has a degree of nine points; because the person has the necessary amount of money and the possibility of making the purchase online and receiving the product the next day. The only thing missing is to perform the action of purchase (which requires a very low level of physical and mental effort), but both resources are highly viable, almost immediately. The third option has a viability level of ten points; because it is available immediately, without an effort.

Options of manifestation		Level of viability
1	Buying a new laptop	(+) 9
2	Buying a video game console	(+) 9
3	Leaving the money in the bank	(+) 10

Figure 67: Level of viability of the options. Case 1.

Given the equivalence between the equation of real well-being and the equation of real valuation, each option has the following values:

Options of manifestation		Projected well-being	Viability	Equation of real well-being	Real well-being
1	Having a new laptop	(+) 9	(+) 9	$9 - (10 - 9) = 8$	(+) 8
2	Having a video game console	(+) 7	(+) 9	$7 - (10 - 9) = 6$	(+) 6
3	Leaving the money in the bank	(+) 2	(+) 10	$2 - (10 - 10) = 2$	(+) 2

Figure 68: Calculation of the real well-being of the options. Case 1.

In figure 68, after calculating the level of real well-being that the person feels from each one of these options, and following the law of decision, we can deduce that she will choose option 1, because it is the one that offers her the highest relative level of real well-being.

As a consequence, according to the law of rational behavior, that option will turn into a need for this person, which she will seek to satisfy through a series of organized behaviors that she will plan and execute to achieve the manifestation of the projected result.

Case 2:

A person imagines himself owning a luxury car (car A), and this option offers him a degree of well-being of ten points. Then, he imagines himself owning a less luxurious car (car B), which offers him a degree of well-being of seven points, in comparison. His third option is an economy car (car C), which offers him a degree of well-being of five points, since it is worse than the first option, but much better than the fourth option. The fourth option is not buying a car and keep using the public transport, which makes him feel a level of ill-being of six points.

Projected options		Level of valuation/ well-being	Hierarchic order
1	Car A	(+) 10	Option 1
2	Car B	(+) 7	Option 2
3	Car C	(+) 5	Option 3
4	Not buying a car	(-) 6	Option 4

Figure 69: Valuation structure. Case 2.

If we want to know which purchase decision he will make, we must see how he evaluates the probability of materializing these options.

Car A is so expensive, that he considers it inviable, with a level of inviability of ten points. In other words, the external constraint (obtaining the amount of money that would allow him to buy it) is deemed to be insuperable.

Car B is less expensive, but there is still a monetary constraint, which the person considers superable, but subject to another external constraint: obtaining a bank loan and the possibility of being able to pay that loan in the future. Getting that loan and being able to pay it in due time is deemed probable, but with a low level of probability. For this reason, we could say that this person assigns a level four of viability to this option.

Car C is the most economical one and it is accessible almost immediately, because the person already has that sum of money, and all he has to do is go to a car dealership and buy it. As a consequence, option 3 is assigned a level of viability of nine points.

Option 4 has a level of viability of ten points, since it is already happening. The possibility is already materialized.

Options of manifestation		Level of viability
1	Car A	(-) 10
2	Car B	(+) 4
3	Car C	(+) 9
4	Not buying a car	(+) 10

Figure 70: Level of viability of the options. Case 2.

As we will see below, this is a case in which the level of viability drastically affects the final decision, as a result of altering the hierarchy of valuations that were originally projected.

The person imagines the highest level of well-being with the projected option 1, but he considers it absolutely inviable; therefore, it is not an option that he chooses to materialize.

From the viable options, car B is the most valued one; however, the person will choose to buy car C. The reason for this is that the difference of projected well-being between option 2 and option 3 is lower than the difference between their perceived viability levels. In other words, the marginal degree of well-being produced by imagining himself owning car B in comparison with car C is lower than the difference between the necessary effort to get car B and the necessary effort to get car C. For this person, the viability cost of overcoming the constraints to obtain car B (going to the bank to ask for a loan and incur a debt that he does not know if he will be able to pay) has a level of six points (ten minus four); while the viability cost of buying car C, for which he already has the money, has only one point (it only implies going to the dealership and buying it).

The viability cost of option 2 reduces the level of well-being of the option so much that option 3 takes the first place in the hierarchic order. As a consequence, the person will decide to buy car C, since it is the option that provides him with the highest level of real well-being.

Options of manifestation		Projected well-being	Viability	Equation of real well-being	Real well-being	Hierarchic order
1	Car A	(+) 10	(-) 10	$10 - (10 + 10) = -10$	(-) 10	Option 3
2	Car B	(+) 7	(+) 4	$7 - (10 - 4) = 1$	(+) 1	Option 2
3	Car C	(+) 5	(+) 9	$5 - (10 - 9) = 4$	(+) 4	Option 4
4	Not buying a car	(-) 6	(+) 10	$-6 - (10 - 10) = -6$	(-) 6	Option 1

Figure 71: Calculation of the real well-being of the options. Case 2.

<u>Case 3</u>:

Let us remember the example mentioned in former chapters, in which a person is at the office and imagines three possible activities for his next holidays (resting in the beach, finishing the project he is working on, and fixing his house) assigning them a positive valuation of nine, five, and two points, respectively. Those valuation levels are equivalent to the projected level of well-being for each one of the options.

Projected options		Level of valuation/ well-being	Hierarchic order
1	Resting in the beach	(+) 9	Option 1
2	Finished project	(+) 5	Option 2
3	House fixed	(+) 2	Option 3

Figure 72: Valuation structure. Case 3.

Let us suppose that when the individual performs a viability evaluation of each one of the options, he assigns a level eight of viability to the first one (since he has the resources to carry it out, but they are not immediate, because he has to ask his boss for some days off), a level five of inviability to the second one (because he needs the presence of a coworker to complete the project, and this person is taking days off in those dates), and a level of viability of six points to the third option (the person considers viable to finish fixing his house in those days, but that depends on other intermediate resources that he must still get, which require some time and dedication).

Options of manifestation		Level of viability
1	Resting in the beach	(+) 8
2	Finished project	(-) 5
3	House fixed	(+) 6

Figure 73: Level of viability of the options. Case 3.

Given the equivalence between the equation of real well-being and the equation of real valuation, each option has the following values:

	Options of manifestation	Projected well-being	Viability	Equation of real well-being	Real well-being	Hierarchic order
1	Resting in the beach	(+) 9	(+) 8	9 – (10 – 8) = 7	(+) 7	Option 1
2	Finished project	(+) 5	(-) 5	5 – (10 + 5) = - 10	(-) 10	Option 3
3	House fixed	(+) 2	(+) 6	2 – (10 – 6) = -2	(-) 2	Option 2

Figure 74: Calculation of the real well-being of the options. Case 3.

In this case, after calculating the level of viability, the first option is not almost affected in its level of well-being, since the degree of facileness to materialize the option is high (eight points). This option does not lose its place in the hierarchy, and it is the one that the human system chooses to carry out.

However, we notice that the level of well-being of the second option and the third one becomes negative, because the viability cost surpasses the degree of valuation of the projected options. In addition, the second option now occupies the third place in the hierarchic order, affected by the viability cost.

Case 4:

A person is thinking of changing jobs. Currently, she is working at job A and the idea of continuing in that position causes her a projected ill-being of grade four. As a second option, she has the opportunity of taking a new job of a lower rank in another city (job B), and this idea causes her a projected well-being of two points. At the same time, the option of not working causes her a great degree of ill-being; for this reason, she assigns this option a negative valuation of eight points.

	Projected options	Level of valuation/ well-being	Hierarchic order
1	Job A (current)	(-) 4	Option 2
2	Job B	(+) 2	Option 1
3	Unemployment	(-) 8	Option 3

Figure 75: Valuation structure. Case 4.

As we can see in figure 75, job B has the highest level in her valuation hierarchy. However, when she evaluates the viability cost, the situation changes.

Options of manifestation		Level of viability
1	Job A (current)	(+) 10
2	Job B	(+) 2
3	Unemployment	(+) 8

Figure 76: Level of viability of the options. Case 4.

For this human system, the option of keeping her current job has a degree of viability of ten points, since all she has to do is continuing with the routine she has learned over the years.

On the other hand, the option of taking job B requires a greater effort: she must leave her house and rent a new one, move her whole family to another city, and adapt to the new company and the new tasks. This option has a delayed viability and requires overcoming a series of constraints. As a consequence, it has a degree of viability of two points.

Finally, the option of not working has a medium-term viability (because she has savings to do it for a while, and her spouse also has an income), with a viability level of eight points.

	Options of manifestation	Projected well-being	Viability	Equation of real well-being	Real well-being	Hierarchic order
1	Job A (current)	(-) 4	(+) 10	$-4 - (10 - 10) = -4$	(-) 4	Option 1
2	Job B	(+) 2	(+) 2	$2 - (10 - 2) = -6$	(-) 6	Option 2
3	Unemployment	(-) 8	(+) 8	$-8 - (10 - 8) = -10$	(-) 10	Option 3

Figure 77: Calculation of the real well-being of the options. Case 4.

As we can see in figure 77, the degree of real well-being of the three options turns out being negative. As a result, the person will choose the option that minimizes the level of real ill-being. In other words, she will decide to continue with her current job. This happens because, in spite of the ill-being generated daily by her current job, the option of changing jobs is very expensive, and the option of being unemployed causes her a higher level of ill-being (even when it is highly viable).

Before concluding, it is worth making some **clarifications**:

1.   The results obtained are values that represent a hypothetical state of well-being or ill-being. They are useful for comparing the real weightings of the options.

The equation of real well-being contains hypothetical, relative and subjective values of the projected levels of well-being (or ill-being) and of the viability costs. These numbers are the ones that determine which option is more valuable than another, hence, which option the person will choose to manifest. For this reason, this equation is essential in the decision making process. We know that the human system will always choose the option that offers the highest level of well-being or the lowest level of ill-being; that is why it is so useful to compare the results of the different options.

2.   The human system is always experiencing an emotion, positive or negative, there is no neutrality.

When the result of the subtraction for an option is zero, it is considered to cause some level of ill-being. This happens because there is no incentive to carry out the action, since the viability cost has completely nullified the level of well-being. When the viability cost is equivalent to the projected level of well-being, it already causes ill-being; that is why the result tends to be negative. In these cases, the human system perceives that the option is at the threshold of ill-being; thus, by convention, the option is assigned a minus one.

3.   If there is a tie among the options, the human system will tend to add new factors to the analysis. The inactivity caused by the equivalence of values is overcome considering new data.

For example, a person faces two options: "I will go" (option 1) and "I will not go" (option 2), with real values of five and five, respectively. When faced with the momentary indecision, the mind continues to emit thoughts, such as: "if I go, perhaps something different will happen," "maybe I will meet someone special," and "I have not been out for a long time." With these new thoughts, the final values are altered until the person makes the decision.

Inevitably, the human system starts evaluating information that will end up changing the real values of the projected well-being or the projected ill-being. As a consequence, there will always be a difference that will cause the person to make a decision.

The equations continue being solved, until the subject chooses. This reasoning process is repeated until the equivalence is overcome, which means that a difference is generated. When this difference is generated, the option that offers the greatest benefit (that is, the one that offers the highest level of relative well-being or the lowest level of relative ill-being) will prevail. That option will be the one chosen by the human system.

Let us remember that the mental system is constantly receiving stimuli. There may be a moment of temporary equivalence, but the system does not remain inactive; instead, it continues adding and evaluating data. When new information is added, the relative level of well-being (or ill-being) is altered, and the indecision is resolved.

There is never a situation of no decision. Because even if, in the face of a tie, the human system decides to abandon the list of options, there is a decision to do nothing (or to evaluate new options and discard the previous ones).

4.   The equation of real well-being is a hypothetical calculation that highlights the complex evaluation that the human system performs to make a decision. The criteria involved in the decision making process are countless, but this complexity has been simplified. The equation is a simplification of reality, which serves to understand the decision making process in an elegant way.

The valuation structure is constantly altered. In this evaluation, we are "freezing a moment;" it is the "photograph of a second." From an enormous number of decisions, we take the picture of one decision.

This is the maximum level of elegance that we can offer when it comes to analyzing the reasons why a subject decides, that is, why it chooses that option and not another one. It is a mathematical way to show that the person will choose the option that offers the lowest possible level of ill-being or the highest possible level of well-being.

5.   The human system will not choose options of insuperable inviability, even when their level of valuation is very high. However, evaluating the options of insuperable inviability can help the person to contemplate ways of turning them into viable options.

6.   A map of the level of projected well-being/ill-being and the level of projected viability/inviability (see figure 78) may add more information for the decision making, allowing the human system to reevaluate the options before deciding.

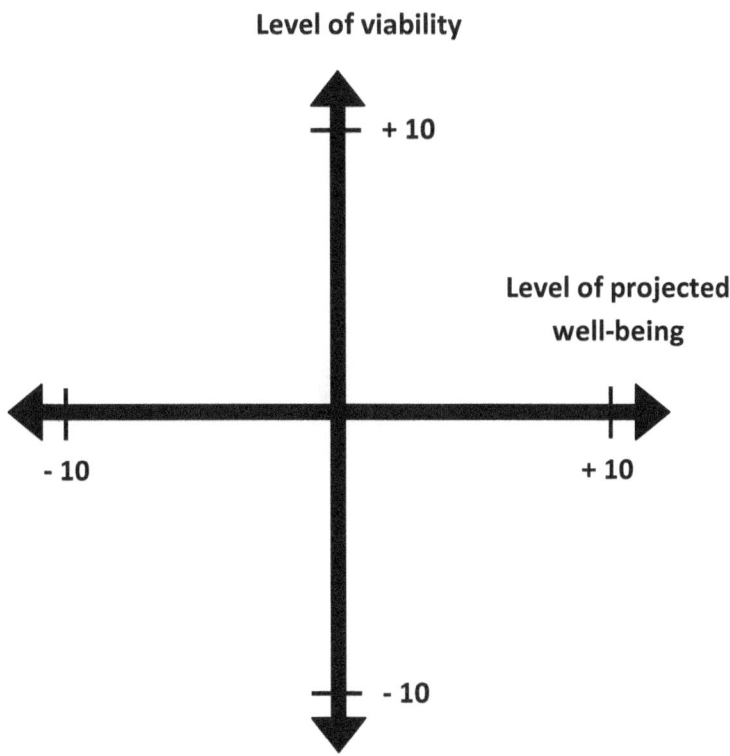

Figure 78: Map of real well-being.

The vertical axis shows the degree of viability/inviability, and the horizontal axis shows the degree of projected well-being/projected ill-being for each one of the options.

The human system can alter the results, seeking to increase the levels of viability of an option or working with its belief system to modify the level of valuation of the options. For the first alternative, the map of resources and constraints (figure 48) is very useful. For the second alternative, the study of the belief system is of vital importance.

CONCLUSION

In the decision systems theory, we have followed a schematic path that emphasized the existence of a mental program responsible for all the decisions that the human system executes.

This program is a belief subsystem called decision system, which, in turn, is formed by two subsystems: the valuation system and the viability evaluation system.

The valuation system is constituted by associations of valuation beliefs that are responsible for decoding the sensory stimuli and turning them into weighting judgments about diverse elements of reality.

The viability evaluation system is constituted by associations of viability beliefs, which are responsible for decoding the sensory stimuli and turning them into viability or inviability judgments about the different options that the protagonist contemplates.

From the interaction of the weighting judgments and the viability judgments about a certain set of options, the system will determine which one is, relatively and subjectively, the most appreciated or the least depreciated (if all the options have a negative valuation).

The options are subject to various mental processes that have been expressed throughout this book and whose elegant and simplified formula has been the decision system, which is the one that receives the input of sensory stimuli and generates decisions as an emergent property.

Human systems choose by mental mechanisms, but the vast majority does not recognize them. The understanding of these mechanisms allow us to comprehend why a particular person chooses one option instead of another.

We have found several postulates, and it would not make sense to repeat them here, since they are well detailed in the book. Nevertheless, it is important to highlight, according to the author's criteria, the following phenomena: the self-esteem equation and the equation of real well-being.

The comprehension of the value correlations that constitute a person's particular self-esteem equation enables us to understand, to a great extent, why some types of capital and some events are more appreciated than others. The teleology manifested in this equation, which is the search for self-esteem through the attainment of certain lifestyles, leads the human systems to contemplate endogenous and exogenous factors (which enable them and restrict them) and, consequently, to decide how to proceed to satisfy it according to their particular decision criteria.

The equation of real well-being is the closure of the entire work. It is the mathematization of a reasoning process that contemplates how all the projected valuations, derived from and equivalent to the projected emotions in relation to certain options, face the viability cost, which can modify the projected emotions about the contemplated options due to the relative presence or absence of resources and constraints.

The projection of the emotional experience in relation to an option is altered, in general, when the protagonist is confronted with the reality and its circumstances. The option that, at the beginning and in its purest form, offered a relatively high level of well-being (and, therefore, an equivalent level of positive valuation) may suffer certain changes in its initial values when faced with the viability evaluation, and the person may conclude that the real level of well-being is not the one initially projected.

Human systems use this cognitive mechanism to determine the real, subjective values offered by each one of the options compared and will proceed to choose the one that maximizes their level of well-being or minimizes their level of ill-being, depending on the situation.

In summary, people choose the options that offer them the highest relative level of real well-being or the lowest relative level of real ill-being, as a result of a cognitive process that contrasts the emotional projection with the viability cost.

This mental operation, usually unconscious for the vast majority of human systems, is the one performed by the decision system. The thorough analysis of this particular belief subsystem will allow us to understand the origin of individual and collective human behaviors, something that I consider absolutely necessary for the disciplines of humanities and social sciences.

Thank you very much for your attention.

GLOSSARY

Active belief subsystem: Set of associations of beliefs responsible for generating certain thought patterns.

Active belief system: Entity that justifies its existence and functions as a whole through the interaction of the active belief subsystems.

Active beliefs: Set of beliefs that have an effect on the thinking process and, therefore, on the resulting thoughts.

Anticapital: Negative factor of reality that, when possessed and accumulated, increases the level of negative self-valuation of its owner.

Appreciative thoughts: Thoughts that manifest a positive valuation of different aspects of reality. Valuation thoughts with a positive pole.

Artificial systems: Entity that justifies its existence and functions as a whole through the interaction of the industrial systems and the educational systems. Also called "technological systems."

Association of beliefs: Set of beliefs that are connected to each other by certain logical principles and are responsible for generating certain thoughts.

Behavior: Corporal action (physical and/or linguistic) that affects reality.

Belief: Idea that has a certain energetic charge and intensity and possess a certain degree of veracity.

Belief system: Subsystem that belongs to the mental system. Entity that justifies its existence and functions as a whole through the interaction of beliefs. The input of the belief system are sensory images, and the output are thoughts.

Capital: Factor which is positively valued by the human system and, when obtained and incremented, contributes to increasing the person's self-esteem.

Choosing: Deciding.

Collective human system: Social system. Community.

Compete: To perform an action in order to obtain a relatively superior valuation in relation to one or more positively valued factors.

Consciousness: Ability of the soul to recognize the processes of the mental system and the body system.

Constraints: Restrictions on the human systems' actions and, therefore, on their possibilities of manifestation.

Corporal action: Movement performed by a human system through its body system. Corporal actions can be physical and/or linguistic.

Corroboration: Empirical evidence that supports the justification.

Criteria: Associations of normative beliefs that enable the assignment of diverse linguistic meanings to a certain set of sensory images that are logically connected with them. Set of rules that determine the different types of evaluations according to the different sensory stimuli that the human system perceives.

Criteria of external inviability: Associations of beliefs responsible for identifying the external constraints that restrict the human system in the attainment of the option it is contemplating.

Criteria of external valuation: Associations of beliefs that contribute to the validation, or not, to some degree, of the factors that constitute the human system's external reality.

Criteria of external viability: Associations of beliefs responsible for detecting the external resources that enable the human system to manifest the option it is contemplating.

Criteria of internal inviability: Associations of beliefs responsible for identifying the internal constraints that limit the human system's manifestation of the option it is contemplating.

Criteria of internal valuation: Associations of beliefs that contribute to the validation, or not, to some degree, of the factors that constitute the human system's internal reality.

Criteria of internal viability: Associations of beliefs responsible for detecting the internal resources that enable the human system to manifest the option it is contemplating.

Criteria of inviability: Associations of normative beliefs that determine the diverse inviability judgments about certain phenomena of the human system's reality.

Criteria of self-valuation: Criteria of internal valuation.

Criteria of valuation: Associations of normative valuation beliefs that constitute the valuation subsystems and contribute to generating several valuation judgments about the different elements of reality that define the human system and its environment.

Criteria of viability: Associations of normative beliefs that determine the diverse viability judgments about certain phenomena of the human system's reality.

Criteria of viability evaluation: Set of criteria that includes the criteria of viability and the criteria of inviability.

Current way of life: Set of endogenous and exogenous factors that define the human system's present lifestyle.

Data: Sensory images that proceed from the human systems' internal or external reality, decoded according to their particular active belief system.

Deciding: Mental action by which human systems determine the options of manifestation, which are restricted or enabled by certain endogenous and exogenous factors, and select the one they consider the most valuable according to their structure of preferences.

Decision: Projective thought that determines the future corporal actions that the human system will perform.

Decision criteria: Set of criteria that includes the criteria of valuation and the criteria of viability evaluation.

Decision system: Subsystem that belongs to the belief system. Entity that justifies its existence and functions as a whole through the interaction of the valuation system and the viability evaluation system. The input are sensory images, and the output are decisions.

Degree of difficulty: Relative magnitude of constraints that restrict a human system to materialize a certain option.

Degree of facileness: Relative magnitude of resources that enable a human system to materialize a certain option.

Degree of inviability: Degree of relative difficulty to get the option evaluated by the human system.

Degree of viability: Degree of relative facileness to get the option evaluated by the human system.

Derogatory thoughts: Thoughts that manifest a negative valuation of different aspects of reality. Valuation thoughts with a negative pole.

Desired way of life: Set of endogenous and exogenous factors that define the human system's desired lifestyle.

Ecological systems: Natural systems.

Emotion: Sensation that occurs in the body system as a result of bio-sensorially recognizing the structure of a thought. Also called "feeling."

Emotional ill-being: Manifestation of different types of negative emotions of different energetic intensities. Also called "ill-being."

Emotional well-being: Manifestation of different types of positive emotions of different energetic intensities. Also called "well-being."

Endogenous factors: Set of constraints and resources, originated in the human system's internal reality, which respectively restrict it and enable it.

Endogenous systems: Systems that define the human systems' internal reality.

Energetic intensity: Amount of mental energy contained in a belief, a thought, or an emotion.

Energetic pole: Energetic charge assumed by a belief, thought, or emotion. It can be either positive or negative.

Environment: External reality with which the human system interacts.

Esteem: To appreciate, or to positively value, a certain phenomenon.

Evaluation: Assignment of characteristics to the judged phenomenon according to the criteria employed by the evaluating human system.

Exogenous factors: Set of constraints and resources, originated in the human system's external reality, which respectively restrict it and enable it.

Exogenous systems: All the systems that are part of the protagonist human system's environment and, therefore, are capable of affecting it. They can be divided into natural systems, artificial systems, and state systems.

External coherence: Degree of associative logic that exists between the analyzed data and the phenomena of reality that they represent.

External reality: Set of phenomena that happen in the human system's environment.

External valuation system: Subsystem that belongs to the valuation system. Entity that justifies its existence and functions as a whole through the interaction of the positive and negative criteria of external valuation. It determines the mechanism by which the human system assigns weightings, positive or negative, to the different elements of its external reality.

External viability evaluation system: Subsystem that belongs to the viability evaluation system. Entity that justifies its existence and functions as a whole through the interaction of the criteria of viability and inviability regarding the external reality of the protagonist human system. Also called "external viability system."

External viability system: External viability evaluation system.

Fidelity: Degree of relative accuracy that certain information possesses.

Formal socialization process: Socialization process that derives from the formal educational system.

Free will: Ability of the soul to choose among different options of manifestation.

Freedom: Faculty of the soul that enables the possibility of choosing among different options of manifestation.

Human system: Entity that justifies its existence and functions as a whole through the interaction of the soul, the mental system, and the body system.

Idea: Sensory images with a certain linguistic meaning, composed of one or more words that assume a logical grammatical sense.

Individual human system: Human being.

Individual person: Individual human system endowed with an identity.

Informal socialization process: Socialization process that derives from the informal educational system.

Information: Set of data about different phenomena that can have several levels of fidelity.

Internal coherence: Degree of associative logic of the ideas that constitute the analyzed data.

Internal evaluation system: Internal viability evaluation system.

Internal reality: Set of phenomena that happen within the human system. Internal reality can be divided into internal mental reality and internal physical reality.

Internal valuation system: Subsystem that belongs to the valuation system. Entity that justifies its existence and functions as a whole through the interaction of the positive and negative criteria of self-valuation. It determines the mechanism by which the human system assigns weightings, positive or negative, to different aspects of its internal reality. Also called "self-valuation system."

Internal viability evaluation system: Subsystem that belongs to the viability evaluation system. Entity that justifies its existence and functions as a whole through the interaction of the criteria of viability and inviability regarding the internal reality of the protagonist human system. Also called "internal viability system."

Inviability: Improbability that a human system will be able to materialize a certain objective, according to the endogenous and exogenous systems that enable it and restrict it. If the inviability is insuperable, it is deemed as absolute. If the inviability is superable, it can be evaluated according to different degrees.

Irrational behavior: Physical and/or linguistic action, developed on the basis of certain decision criteria that possess a certain level of inaccuracy.

Irrationality: Degree of inaccuracy of the decision criteria that the human system employs for the development of several teleological behaviors.

Judgment: Evaluation of a certain phenomenon made by the human system on the basis of certain type of information.

Justification: Argumentative explanation, logically developed, that supports a criterion.

Linguistic action: Word and/or phrase manifested by a human system through an expression that is oral, written, gestural, or a combination of all three.

Linguistic meaning: Coherent grammatical articulation in accordance with the human system's operative language. One of the elements that constitute beliefs and thoughts (the other elements are sensory images, pole, and intensity).

Logical principles: Ideas that guide the development of information in accordance with certain rational parameters.

Mental action: Activity performed by a human system in its mental system.

Mental sensory system: Subsystem that belongs to the mental system. Entity that justifies its existence and functions as a whole through the interaction of the auditory, visual, tactile, olfactory, gustatory, and internal sensitive subsystems. It is the entity in charge of capturing sensory information and converting it into sensory images.

Mental system: Entity that justifies its existence and functions as a whole through the interaction of the mental sensory system and the belief system.

The input of the mental system is sensory information and the output are thoughts.

Natural systems: Entity that justifies its existence and functions as a whole through the interaction of the geographic, oceanic, climatic, and biological systems. Also called "ecological systems."

Needs: What the human system lacks of and wishes to satisfy.

Passive beliefs: Set of beliefs that are in a potential state, and for that reason they do not affect the thinking process, nor the thoughts that derive from it.

Perceiving: The act of capturing the events of reality through the use of the senses.

Person: Human system endowed with an identity.

Personality: Active belief system.

Physical action: Any non-linguistic, corporal action performed by a human system.

Preferring: The act of assigning more weight to an option, compared with another or others.

Projective thoughts: Thoughts about the future that anticipate the actions that the human system will execute.

Protagonist: Human system that is being analyzed.

Rational behavior: Physical and/or linguistic action, developed on the basis of certain decision criteria that possess a certain level of fidelity.

Rationality: Degree of fidelity of the decision criteria that the human system employs for the development of several teleological behaviors.

Reality: Set of phenomena that happen.

Relative relevance: Amount of weighting that is altered according to the elements that are being compared and evaluated, subject to the criteria of a certain valuation system.

Resources: Means that enable the development of certain actions.

Result: Modification of reality generated by behavior.

Risk: Probability that an expectation, expressed through an end, is not fulfilled.

Self-esteem: Act and effect of valuating oneself positively, performed by a human system.

Self-esteem equation: Set of associated valuation criteria that determine the hierarchy of valuations, needs, and ends which guide human behavior to preserve and increase the human system's self-esteem

Self-valuation system: Internal valuation system.

Sensory images: Mental sensory reproductions based on the senses of the biological system of perception. They are the output of the mental sensory system and the input of the belief system. One of the elements that constitute beliefs and thoughts (the other elements are linguistic meaning, pole, and intensity). Also called "sensory impressions."

Sensory impressions: Sensory images.

Sensory stimuli: Unified fragments of sensory information perceived by the receiving human system, that come from its internal or external reality and trigger the gestation of sensory images.

Social person: Collective human system endowed with an identity.

Social system: Entity that justifies its existence and functions as a whole through the interaction of two or more individual human systems. Entity that justifies its existence and functions as a whole through the interaction of the social will, the social mental system, and the social body system. Also called "community" and "collective human system."

Socialization process: Phenomenon by which the members of a social system are educated to make their respective belief structures compatible with the belief structure of the community.

Soul: Conscious energy that enjoys free will and operates on the mental system and on the body system. Also called "will."

State systems: Entity that justifies its existence and functions as a whole through the interaction of the political systems and the civil systems.

Structure of ends: Structure of teleological judgments that are hierarchically organized according to the relative valuations that have been assigned to them. Also called "hierarchy of ends."

Structure of needs: Structure of judgments of necessity that are hierarchically organized according to the relative amount of weighting assigned to them. Also called "hierarchy of needs."

Technological systems: Artificial systems.

Technology: Set of knowledge and techniques that enable the development of certain industries and their related goods.

Thought: Idea that possesses a certain energetic charge and intensity that affects the body system. It is the emergent property of the belief system and the mental system.

Thoughts that command behavior: Thoughts responsible for ordering the body to execute behaviors that materialize projective thoughts.

Valuating: Assigning a certain degree of relative value, positive or negative, to each element of the perceived reality.

Valuation: Act and effect of valuating.

Valuation structure: Structure of valuation judgments that are hierarchically organized according to the relative amount of weighting that the valuation system assigned to the different stimuli. Also called "valuation hierarchy."

Valuation system: Belief subsystem that assigns a certain degree of relative value, positive or negative, to each element of the perceived reality. Entity that justifies its existence and functions as a whole through the interaction of the internal valuation subsystem and external valuation subsystem. The input are sensory images, and the output are valuation thoughts.

Valuation thoughts: Thoughts that manifest a valuation of different aspects of reality. Also called "valuation judgments."

Value: Degree of relative relevance, positive or negative, that the human system assigns to certain elements of reality.

Value correlations: Programed sequence of phenomena that contribute to the satisfaction of a certain human system's self-esteem equation.

Viability: Probability that a human system will be able to materialize a certain objective, according to the endogenous and exogenous systems that enable it and restrict it. There are different degrees of viability.

Viability evaluation system: Belief subsystem in charge of estimating the degree of viability or inviability of the contemplated options. Entity that justifies its existence and functions as a whole through the interaction of the internal viability evaluation system and the external viability evaluation system. The input are sensory images, and the output are viability judgments. Also called "viability system."

Viability system: Viability evaluation system.

Way of life: Set of constraints and resources that, respectively, restrict and enable a human system.

Will: Soul.

INDEX OF FIGURES

ABOUT THE AUTHOR

Juan Martín Figini is the author of a series of innovative theories that offer an original model about the functioning of the mind and its effects on the particular manifestation of each human system at the level of beliefs, thoughts, emotions, behaviors, and social relationships.

In the year 2018, he published the book *Mental Systems Theory. New and Expanded Edition*, which is a modified and more comprehensive version of the *Mental Systems Theory* (published in 2012 and 2009).

In the years 2016 and 2017, he published the following books in Spanish: *Teoría de los Sistemas Mentales, Teoría de los Sistemas Sociales. Un modelo basado en los Sistemas Mentales* (Social Systems Theory. A model based on Mental Systems), *Teoría de los Sistemas de Decisión* (Decision Systems Theory), and *Rousseau: alienación, falsa identidad y el rol social del líder consciente* (Rousseau: alienation, false identity and the social role of the conscious leader).

He has developed the Mental Systems Engineering, a discipline that enables to understand and to operate on the mental system, in order to align the human systems' belief structure with their desired state. Applying this methodology, he has designed and facilitated a set of consulting and training programs in several countries, in the areas of psychology, social studies, politics, business, education, and sports, such as "Vocational Development," "Mental Training for Athletes," and "Personal Evolution," among others.

He worked as a Consultant for Manchester Business School, The University of Manchester, UK. He has developed and delivered several educational programs for the British Council, such us "Successful Teamwork" and "Words create Worlds."

He has a Degree in Political Science from Saint Andrew's University (Argentina). His degree thesis, titled: *Alienation in Rousseau: Social Criticism and Pedagogical Project*, received from the academic jury of Saint Andrew's University the maximum score of ten points. He also studied the International Relations Degree in that university.

He was granted a complete scholarship by the Case Western Reserve University, USA, where he obtained the Post-graduate Degree: Appreciative Inquiry Certificate in Positive Business and Society Change.

He has a Post-graduate Degree in Models and Tools of Ontological Coaching and a Post-graduate Degree in Techniques and Dynamics of Coaching Intervention, from the University of Buenos Aires (Argentina). He holds a Master's Degree in Neuro-Linguistic Programming, from the Southern Institute of NLP, The Society of NLP, International NLP (USA). He received the International Certificate in Coaching from the International Coaching Community (ICC), where he was evaluated and approved by Joseph O'Connor. He was certified in the Fundamental Course and the Advance Level of the Emotional Freedom Techniques (EFT), from the EFT Certificate of Completion Program (USA).

Currently, he is developing a series of books based on the *Mental Systems Theory* and the *Social Systems Theory*, with applicability in different areas of the humanities and social sciences, such as the Educational Systems Theory and the Political Systems Theory, among others.

www.juanmartinfigini.com

RELATED WORKS

The following books complement the study of the *Decision Systems Theory. A model based on Mental Systems.* They have been referenced throughout this work, and they have been written by Juan Martín Figini.

Books published:

- *Mental Systems Theory. New and Expanded Edition.* Figini, Juan Martín. Authorhouse, 2018.

- *Teoría de los Sistemas Sociales. Un modelo basado en los Sistemas Mentales.* Figini, Juan Martín. Authorhouse, 2017.

- *Teoría de los Sistemas de Decisión. Un modelo basado en los Sistemas Mentales.* Figini, Juan Martín. Authorhouse, 2017.

- *Teoría de los Sistemas Mentales.* Figini, Juan Martín. Authorhouse, 2016.

Next books*:

- *Social Systems Theory*
  A model based on Mental Systems

- *Political Systems Theory*
  A model based on Mental and Social Systems

- *Educational Systems Theory*
  A model based on Mental and Social Systems

- *Mental Systems Engineering*

* The books mentioned in this list will be published soon.

www.juanmartinfigini.com